CODE NAME: PALE HORSE

CODE NAME: PALE HORSE

HOW I WENT UNDERCOVER TO EXPOSE AMERICA'S NAZIS

SCOTT PAYNE

WITH MICHELLE SHEPHARD

ATRIA BOOKS

New York • Amsterdam/Antwerp • London
Toronto • Sydney/Melbourne • New Delhi

An Imprint of Simon & Schuster, LLC
1230 Avenue of the Americas
New York, NY 10020

First Atria Books hardcover edition March 2025

ATRIA BOOKS and colophon are trademarks of Simon & Schuster, LLC

For information about special discounts for bulk purchases, please contact Simon & Schuster Special Sales at 1-866-506-1949 or business@simonandschuster.com.

The Simon & Schuster Speakers Bureau can bring authors to your live event. For more information or to book an event, contact the Simon & Schuster Speakers Bureau at 1-866-248-3049 or visit our website at www.simonspeakers.com.

Interior design by Dana Sloan.

Manufactured in the United States of America

1 3 5 7 9 10 8 6 4 2

Library of Congress Cataloging-in-Publication Data

Names: Payne, Scott (FBI agent), author. | Shephard, Michelle, author.
Title: Code name: Pale Horse : how I went undercover to expose America's Nazis / Scott Payne and Michelle Shephard.
Description: New York : Atria Books, [2024] | Includes bibliographical references and index.
Identifiers: LCCN 2023055742 | ISBN 9781668032909 (hardcover) | ISBN 9781668032916 (paperback) | ISBN 9781668032923 (ebook)
Subjects: LCSH: Payne, Scott (FBI agent), | United States. Federal Bureau of Investigation. | White supremacy movements—United States—Case studies. | Neo-Nazism—United States—Case studies. | Hate crimes—United States—Case studies. | Undercover operations—United States—Case studies. | BISAC: POLITICAL SCIENCE / Political Ideologies / Conservatism & Liberalism | HISTORY / United States / 21st Century
Classification: LCC E184.A1 P364 2024 | DDC 335.60973—dc23/eng/20240118
LC record available at https://lccn.loc.gov/2023055742

ISBN 978-1-6680-3290-9
ISBN 978-1-6680-3292-3 (ebook)

To my loving wife and daughters

CONTENTS

CODE NAME: PALE HORSE

PROLOGUE

Rome, Georgia
August 2, 2019

It was a sweltering summer day, the kind of day when it's hard to think about anything but the heat. I was in the Southern town of Rome, Georgia, located in the foothills of the Appalachians. Basically, I was in the middle of nowhere—and I was all alone.

As an undercover employee for the Federal Bureau of Investigation (FBI UCE) I knew backup was usually not far away. At the very least, a team would have known my whereabouts, whether they could reach me or not. Most of the time, though, you had to be self-sufficient in the field, relying solely on your wits and your cover story. And right there, on that hot, humid road, I was "Scott Anderson," a South Carolina biker, former skinhead, and a recruit auditioning to become a member of "The Base."

The Base was one of the fastest-rising, most radical white supremacist groups operating in the U.S. They had only been formed a year before, in 2018, but they were quickly gaining American supporters, and cells were popping up around the world. They were domestic terrorists trying to incite a race war. They wanted society to collapse so they could establish a white ethno-state.

We'd been tracking their online posts on the dark web, and on apps like Telegram and Gab, which included propaganda such as:

- "No need to wait until conditions for revolution exist—guerrilla insurrection can create them. Insurgency begins as a terrorist campaign."
- "If you want a society with traditional values, electoral politics could still achieve that theoretically. But if you want a White society, electoral politics can't achieve that unless the current System of government is replaced. The current System can't be replaced peacefully."

I needed them to trust me and to like me. I needed to get on the inside.

Before coming to Georgia, I had only spoken with members online. They vetted me enough that I got invited to an encrypted chat room. They knew me as "WhiteWarrior88," and I didn't know anyone's real identity.

Over the next week I began chatting with various members, trying to ingratiate myself. Then I got the chance for more. A member going by the name "TMB" invited me to meet some local members in Rome, Georgia, that upcoming weekend.

That's why I was there on August 2. It was my first face-to-face meeting, so they could vet me in person.

I had been given instructions to park, get out of my truck, and locate the town's *Roman Wolf* sculpture. The infamous statue, known more formally as *The Capitoline Wolf*, is a replica of the original art in Rome,

Italy. It depicts a she-wolf suckling the mythical twin founders of Rome: Romulus and Remus. I'd never heard of the sculpture or even the myth before this meeting. But I had heard the name, "Roman Wolf." It was the fake name the leader of The Base gave to himself.

I couldn't find a parking spot in the area they had told me about, which was fine, as driving around gave me chance to scout and see if anyone was following me. I spotted the statue as I searched, so I took a quick picture and sent it to TMB.

Finally, I parked my truck in an open spot behind a coffee shop and texted TMB where I was. He sent a text back that he was watching and soon after two guys approached me. I was the first to talk.

"Are you TMB?" I asked.

One of them nodded.

TMB stood for "The Militant Buddhist," and he was very active on the dark web, where he lurked. We didn't know TMB's real identity or anything at all about him up to this point, except that he was spouting pretty radical things online. Stuff like how he wanted to create a white ethnostate and kill Jews and African Americans.

In real life, TMB was big and frumpy. Probably about six-foot-two, 220 pounds, with thick glasses and a mop of brown hair that spilled over his forehead. He was with another guy who went by the online name of "Pestilence." Pestilence was smaller, about five-ten, 180, and was wearing eight-inch combat boots with his pants bloused in them and a black metal tank top.

The three of us were sizing each other up, boxers in the ring at the beginning of a match. At six-foot-four and 262 pounds, I was larger, but almost double their age, and wondering how the hell this was going to go.

Before we talked further, TMB looked at me warily and said, "Put your phone on airplane mode." I did as he instructed.

Then he pulled out something I had never seen before in my two decades in law enforcement. It looked like some sort of Geiger counter, and he began to pass it all over my body. Presumably, he was trying to pick up a wire, which, thankfully, I was not wearing. But without another word, he walked around my truck, and my pulse quickened.

The device sprang to life, vibrating and making all kinds of racket.

Beep. Beep. BEEP.

It got louder and more frequent, a manic symphony of noise building in intensity the farther he walked.

I knew he was getting close to the GPS tracking device my FBI cover team had just installed. My mind was racing, but I continued to stand there quietly, showing no expression. My only movement was to subtly start dropping my right leg back, to prepare for a fight.

Suddenly, Pestilence spoke up and suggested, "Maybe it's the power lines?"

We were parked on a bit of a hill, and the power lines *were* close to the ground. I could have hugged Pestilence at that moment, but I continued to stand there trying to look bored.

TMB nodded and moved away from my truck. Thankfully, the device in his hand went mad once again and TMB cursed. "Fuck. Yeah, the damn power lines. Okay, follow us and we'll go to another location."

I said "Cool," even though I didn't feel it at all. But I knew I had a second to relax—crisis averted for now. I inhaled through my nose, held it, and then exhaled slowly, trying to bring my heart rate down.

Back alone in my truck, I fumbled to turn on my cell phone, and then without moving my lips, not sure who was watching me, I told the team, "Turn the tracker off." My cover team debated the move, worried they couldn't remotely turn it back on once it was off. I was trying my best to stay calm, channeling a ventriloquist and following TMB's car to the new location as I insisted to the team that it wasn't optional. *Turn it off or this is gonna be the shortest undercover operation I've ever done.* My cover team finally got the point.

TMB and Pestilence slowed their truck and turned into an abandoned concrete plant. The sky had darkened as we drove, and by the time I stepped outside my truck there was a torrential downpour. It all felt like a cliché Hollywood scene. I mean, who doesn't die in a storm, in an abandoned concrete plant, in half of the action movies you've seen? The rain and cloud cover also meant the FBI surveillance plane was now of no use. No GPS. No air support.

Now I was *really* alone.

TMB started with that wand again. As he moved it slowly along my truck, the wand didn't make a sound. Then he came back to me, and I stood there with my arms out in a T, getting soaked in the downpour. Still nothing.

TMB got back into his car and told me to follow him to his home. The air-conditioning in my truck sent a blast of cold air over my drenched body. The rain was pounding so hard I couldn't even hear the radio that was blasting metal.

I was in.

—

When the average American thinks of white supremacy, they conjure up an image of the Ku Klux Klan, the guys in the white robes and pointy hats. (The Klan *does* still exist. In 2017, I infiltrated one of the Klan chapters in Alabama. I'll get to that story.)

But the Klan are basically your grandpa's white supremacists, with deep historical roots in this country. What's new today is a much broader white power movement. There are a lot of names and it's hard to sort who's who. A lot of far-right groups get labeled as white supremacists when they're not. Take for instance groups like the Proud Boys, the Boogaloos, or militias like the Wolverine Watchmen or the Oath Keepers. These organizations may have white supremacist members and engage in illegal activities like trying to overthrow the government or kidnap a governor. But they're not part of the movement I'm talking about. Other groups, like the Patriot Front, the Nationalist Socialist Movement, the League of the South, or the Traditionalist Workers Party, are white supremacist groups, and they're definitely dangerous, but they've been around for a while.

Groups like the one I infiltrated, The Base, present a new ideology within the far-right movement. And I think it is the most dangerous and overlooked threat facing us today. They call themselves "accelerationists."

Although "accelerationism" as a concept has been around since the late 1980s, it has never had such a widespread following in the white supremacist community. Those who adhere to it don't believe there's a political solution to solving anything, because Western governments are irrevocably corrupt. What they do believe is that society will eventually collapse, either on its own or from a man-made event, and their goal is to speed that up by sowing chaos and political tensions. To accelerate it. After they help spark a race war, they will move in and create a white ethnostate.

Accelerationists don't support the political establishment, but they do use it to further their goals. They'll vote for extreme candidates—right or left. I know accelerationists who are about as far right as you can get, but who voted for Hillary Clinton. Yup, Hillary Clinton. This is their thinking: Democrats don't support law enforcement and the military, so they believe a Democrat in charge means crime rates will skyrocket, the U.S. will be flooded by immigrants, society will decline, and the country will burn. I know it sounds counterintuitive, but they are also racists who support the Black Lives Matter movement, believing that these protests always turn violent. Accelerationists think, *Bring it on. Let them destroy the cities.*

Accelerationists are not just angry white guys in their basements. They're actively recruiting and radicalizing online. When they meet in person, they hone their skills at outdoor training camps, planning and plotting to target racial minorities and Jews.

I've spent months in their homes, in their cars, at their training camps, and in their heads. I've learned a lot about accelerationism. It's a dark place, and one we as a society all need to be aware of. My hope is to help shine a light on the growing danger these people pose.

To get us there, I'll explain what it's like to live an often-surreal double life as an undercover agent. How you at times must juggle as many as seven phones, while still being available to your family. I can talk intimately about befriending and really connecting with a target for years, knowing that my only mission is to eventually send him to jail. Or what it's like to take down cops who wear the same badge but abide by a fundamentally different code.

My twenty-eight years in law enforcement serves as a road map of some of the most consequential issues our country has faced in the last few decades. Every case taught me something new.

But I've also screwed up and made a lot of mistakes. I'm loud, I'm brash; I'm a "big splash" kind of guy and sometimes that can rub people the wrong way. At times, I know I've been a cocky SOB. Hell, I've even been the reason for new policy in the undercover operations guide.

I've made mistakes in my personal life as well, and those were truly the toughest times. But I always had my faith, and that carried me through. Many times, when things were bad, I would talk with my "small group" from church. They'd lay their hands on me and pray.

Then there was Kara,[1] my rock-solid partner and wife of more than twenty years, along with our two wonderful daughters. I'd like to think I'm the family glue that helps keep us all together, but Kara has always been the foundation of the family.

When we started dating, I was already a narc. A typical late-night conversation might sound like:

What'd you do tonight, honey?

Oh, I just picked up a few hookers and bought some cocaine. How was your day?

Kara may have known she was marrying Scott Payne, and what he did for a living, but how could she really appreciate that she was also marrying law enforcement? I would miss a lot of big moments for her and my girls. No one forced me to do that—I volunteered for most of it. But for them, it wasn't voluntary, and that was hard. When I signed up for this type of work, my whole family signed up, too.

You don't have to go very far back in the FBI's history to learn about undercovers. The Bureau under J. Edgar Hoover didn't have an undercover program. He didn't believe in it and preferred to hire a bunch of clean-cut, clean-living agents. Me with my tats and earrings? I never would have been hired back then.

But on the tails of Hoover's retirement in 1972, the undercover program was born, and twenty-five special agents were assigned: *Here's your cash and your recorder. Now go out and make cases.* Back then, there were no Attorney General Guidelines or policy manuals regulating undercover work. One of those first twenty-five recruits was Joe Pistone, a.k.a. "Donnie Brasco," one of the most legendary undercovers in the history of the Bureau.

I joined the FBI as a "New Agent in Training" on September 27, 1998. The first couple years were spent mainly assisting senior agents on their cases and learning how to become a case agent myself. Because I wasn't yet married and never minded working long hours, I spent a lot of time conducting mind-numbing, tedious surveillance operations. But then in September 2002, I went to Quantico, to the FBI's "undercover certification" school. I clearly remember saying to myself, "Wait. So they are gonna train us all day in class, keep me up all night doing undercover scenarios, then give me drinks and not let me sleep? I've been training for this my whole life!"

One of my instructors was none other than Joe Pistone.

There's a lot you can teach about how to work undercover, but there's also a natural skill set that you just need to possess. Most importantly, you need to be believable, so you try to be as close to the real you as you can. I was Scott, the jovial country biker guy, sometimes with the nicknames of "Big Country," "Tex," or a few others. Depending on the case, I may or may not have had kids, or been married, or have played D-1 football, or been a musician, but you can bet your ass I lifted weights, rode a Harley, and drank Jack Daniel's, no matter what my last name was on any given day. And I've been told I can carry on a conversation with a brick wall and, when I'm done, the wall is my friend.

During most of my career, I was in the Criminal Division, which meant I helped convict gang leaders, drug dealers, human traffickers, and dirty cops. But in 2016, I joined the Joint Terrorism Task Force (JTTF).

The JTTF had been around since 1980 and was established to cover cases of international terrorism (IT), domestic terrorism (DT), and weapons of mass destruction (WMD). But after the September 11, 2001, attacks, the JTTF became a behemoth. Resources were drawn in from all over the FBI for international terrorism investigations. Those were the ones that garnered the big, dramatic headlines. And even fifteen years later, when I joined the squad, international terrorism was the prestige posting for the JTTF. I remember when I was asked by one of the members of management, "Don't you want to be with the big dogs? The big dogs are IT." I remember thinking, *Just you asking me that makes me want to work domestic terrorism even more.*

It wouldn't be long, though, before domestic terrorism started stealing the headlines. One of my first big successes was against the Aryan Nation, the largest white supremacist gang at the time in Tennessee. The case started with just one Aryan Nation member, who was a known felon and was widely reported to possess an illegal firearm. We tailed him, but every damn time we stopped him, he didn't have the gun. During our investigation, however, we learned he was dealing dope, so we used that, and kept throwing the net out further and further. After eighteen months, along with the DEA (Drug Enforcement Administration), we had enough evidence for forty-four indictments of his crew on drug charges. Not every arrest was of a white supremacist, but a lot of them were.

Our takedown came just five months after America had finally woken up to the problem in our midst with the devastating "Unite the Right" rally in Charlottesville, where Nazi flags were on full display, and tiki torch–carrying crowds chanted racist and anti-Semitic slogans. The Virginia governor declared a state of emergency, and hours later a white supremacist rammed his car into a crowd of counterprotesters, killing Heather Heyer and injuring thirty-five other people.

There's always crime all over America: organized crime, gang and gun violence, drug wars—international and domestic. But since the Charlottesville riots, white nationalist violence has doubled and "racially motivated violent extremism," as we called it at the Bureau, has become the fastest-growing domestic terrorism threat.

And now the movement has shifted. A year or so prior to our investigation into The Base, identifying as an accelerationist was considered "cringe." By 2021, about 90 percent of white nationalist groups were accelerationists. That's a terrifying trend, considering these "soldiers" are working hard to create chaos with guerrilla warfare–style attacks. How do you fight that?

After the September 11, 2001, attacks, a bipartisan committee was established to explain just how four planes and an Al Qaeda plot managed to bring the U.S. to her knees.

Among the many disastrous shortcomings the 9/11 Commission report highlighted was this: "The most important failure was one of imagination. We do not believe leaders understood the gravity of the threat."

The threat is different today. I don't have to imagine it—I've seen it up close.

1

HIGH SCHOOL CONFIDENTIAL

Greenville, South Carolina
1988

There are certain skills that can be taught for doing undercover work, along with a couple critical rules that keep it legal.

Never be violent unless it's in self-defense.
Never initiate a criminal plot, or it's entrapment.

But to be *really* effective at undercover work, there's something inherent, which can't be taught.

Looking back, it was in Eastside High School, in Greenville, South Carolina, when I started to realize I had a knack for being a "people person." I had the ability to be accepted by different groups. One early example I remember was in grade 11, at my high school's talent show, where the band I was in performed "Hot for Teacher," and I grabbed my crotch one too many times.

Again, this was the 1980s and I was a pretty good musician by then, for a seventeen-year-old. I could sing, play guitar, and walk onstage with my bandmates full of confidence. But before that school show, our band résumé largely consisted of performing at keg parties. In the eighties, if you grabbed your crotch while singing Van Halen at a kegger, it was hard to go wrong. That talent show was my first time on an actual stage—let alone appearing in front of a sober audience of adults who had come to watch their kids play the violin, tap dance, or execute a simple karate move.

Before we even finished "*Whoa! Got it bad . . . I'm hot for teacher,*" they closed the curtain on us. First thing Monday morning, I was summoned to Vice Principal Lloyd Walker's office.

Now, Mr. Walker, who was a short, balding Black man who always wore a suit, had been on my back ever since I came to high school. If I had to guess, it was because I was a big kid with an attitude to match. I tended to fight against the establishment. I wore sleeveless shirts and fingerless weightlifting gloves and a spiked leather bracelet. You gotta love the eighties.

I entered his office shoulders back, chest out, sputtering protests before he even had a chance to say a word to me. I mean, how many times could I have grabbed my crotch?

But Mr. Walker stayed calm, like a prosecutor just waiting to pounce after the defense had exhausted all their theatrics. He pulled out a video recording of our performance. Today it seems crazy to *not* have something documented, but back then it was a bit of a novelty. It was also an indictment. There I was on the stage, clearly nervous, and I'll bet you I grabbed my crotch every three seconds.

As I let it all sink in, there was no other way to react but to laugh. My defenses crumbled. I mean, I looked ridiculous. "Wow . . . that was really bad," I said. Suddenly, Mr. Walker, my great high school nemesis on the other side of the desk, was laughing too. We began cracking joke after joke, becoming as friendly as a vice principal and student can be.

Over the next year, he often called me back into his office just to chat. Then one day he asked for my help. He described how someone had spray-painted his home and keyed his car—it was hardly a secret, as everyone in our school knew he was being targeted by a student. Mr. Walker asked, "Could you help me find out who did this?"

I guess he saw something in me beyond my ability to share a joke. I wouldn't say I was what you'd call a "popular" kid at the school, but I moved around effortlessly, getting along with any group—the jocks, the musicians, the potheads, the smokers; hell, I could even talk to the Beta Club.

I didn't realize it in the moment (how could I?), but Mr. Walker had given me my *first undercover gig*. It bugged me that someone at our school had done that to him and his family, so I made it my mission to quietly figure out who it was, just getting a bit of intel wherever I was, working the circles.

In the gym: "Hey, you hear what's been going on?" At parties, in the hallways, outside of school, casually asking: "Man, did you hear about what happened to Mr. Walker? I drove by his house." And often, I wouldn't have to say anything at all; just hang around and listen.

It's amazing how much people usually like to talk if you let them. Information is power. Soon I was able to identify one kid who just seemed out of place and didn't engage in the gossip. He was about my age, pretty nondescript. He had a mullet—a popular style at the time—a thin mustache, and I remember him dating a girl who wrote for the yearbook and school newspaper.

Whenever the topic of Mr. Walker came up, he would just look away, and not participate. His silence was the first red flag. His body language was another giveaway. He looked like he wanted to crawl out of his skin.

I heard from others that he had some beef with Mr. Walker—had been punished and wanted retaliation. I never got the kid to confess to me, but I knew it was him.

I had no problem telling Mr. Walker his name and what I had found out. Mr. Walker wasn't a bad guy and didn't deserve what had happened to him.

I liked the feeling of doing the right thing.

—

Music was always an important part of my life, beyond high school "talent" shows. I came by it naturally, born into a musical family on both my mother's and my father's side, although neither of my parents was a professional musician.

My father, who dropped out of school in the tenth grade, was a very successful landscaper. At one point his business had a full retail store and employed two crews to service the wealthy residents of Greenville, South Carolina, where I grew up. My mother was the book-smart one, and later in life became a much-sought-after accountant, who during her time working for high-profile clients uncovered three major cases of embezzlement.

I was their only child. As my mom liked to exclaim, I was "enough for one lifetime!"

Despite their busy work lives, there was always time for music in my home. My mom was good on the guitar, and my dad played a little piano. I had aunts who also played piano and an uncle who was skilled on the guitar and yet *another* uncle who was a bass player and even auditioned for *A Star Is Born*, a TV talent search show popular back then. My family would often tour churches playing and singing gospel music, and there I was listening to them practice, as a little boy sitting in the front pew, taking it all in.

One of my most distinct memories with gospel music was going with my parents as they helped open a new Baptist church with a predominantly Black congregation somewhere in upstate South Carolina. I must have been about nine years old at the time. Suddenly, I was listening to music I'd never heard in a church before. It was just a simple song, a repetition of *Amen, Amen*.

It's hard to explain just how powerful it was to me. It was as if you'd been used to *The Lawrence Welk Show*, and then you go into the next room and discover Ray Charles, Otis Redding, or Aretha Franklin is performing. I was totally transfixed. I couldn't help but to start stomping my leg.

Thanks to experiences like helping open that church, I really didn't notice the segregation that afflicted South Carolina in the 1980s. And I didn't encounter it during my first years of schooling, when I attended a private Christian school. It wasn't until my public high school that I started to see the racial divide firsthand.

I played football for our Eastside Eagles, and I remember one Monday afternoon out on the field after practice, when we were shooting the shit and talking about our previous weekend. My friend Ricky and I started talking about the parties we'd been to. Lamont and Argentina just looked on, shaking their heads. "You'd never take us to one of those parties," one of them said. I think it was Ricky who spoke first. "Hell yeah, we would." Lamont and Argentina were Black. We considered our Eastside Eagle teammates our brothers, no matter their skin color, on the field and off. I really couldn't understand why they thought this was a big deal.

I remember pulling my mom's red four-door Buick Somerset into Lamont and Argentina's neighborhood—a government housing block with a mainly Black population—and we were immediately surrounded by residents asking us what we wanted. I cracked the window. "We're here to pick up Lamont and Argentina," and the mood suddenly shifted, and a call went up for the guys. Soon our teammates were in the back seat and off we went.

I can't remember the name of the neighborhood where the party was held, or even who was hosting it, but I do know it was in a pretty nice part of town. I parked the car, grabbed the beers, and the four of us walked in.

All eyes were immediately on us, and if it had been a scene from a movie, this would have been the moment when the record scratched and the music stopped. We didn't know all the kids there, but we knew a lot of them, and it was immediately clear that Lamont and Argentina were not only unexpected guests, they also weren't welcome. Some kids looked visibly scared.

After a couple awkward conversations, we decided to leave. But the night was young so we didn't stop there. Driving in my mom's Somerset on that warm summer night we went in search of our own fun. *Who needed a house party?* We had each other, and a few twelve-packs in the back seat. We drove to Paris Mountain, which was the place to go on the weekends just to hang out. You'd park by the radio tower and trek down one of the trails until you hit "the rock," where you could relax, drink, and a have a great view of the city.

Problem was, as soon as we neared the top, a South Carolina Highway Patrol checkpoint came into view and there was no way to turn around or swerve to avoid it.

I'll never forget what happened next.

We knew we were done for underage drinking, and the troopers wasted no time in roughing us all up a bit. They weren't beating us, but we were ordered out of the car, hands on the hood, lots of shouting—that kind of stuff. At one point, I had my head slammed on the hood. But then I watched as Lamont and Argentina received a different kind of treatment, filled with racial slurs. Each verbal blow got me madder and madder.

When the trooper kept yelling at me to give him my car keys, that anger built, and I turned, took my hands off the hood, and threw them hard at him, not realizing how close he was. He caught them as they hit his chest, and I thought, *Oh shit. I'm going to go to jail,* and quickly turned around, hands and head back down.

In the end, they let us all go, but not before emptying several beers on the rear driver's side floorboards. Lamont and Argentina were quiet on the ride back down the mountain, and I remember Ricky and me apologizing for what had happened. "It's not your fault," they said. It was clear this wasn't their first experience like this.

It was one of my first real reckonings with racism, and it has stayed with me until today. It would be something that I would revisit over the years, as I examined my own personal beliefs when I infiltrated white supremacist groups, and then most profoundly in 2020, when law enforcement agencies all over America looked inward after the death of George Floyd.

—

I didn't always walk the line growing up. I got in fights, smoked dope, drank a lot, and at times, I didn't associate myself with the best influences.

My childhood had always been blessed and I was surrounded by love and support. But when I was about twelve, my dad suffered from depression and my parents started to argue. It happened pretty suddenly. I had never really seen them fight in my whole life up until then. When I was thirteen, they told me they were separating and that set me down a dark path. People kept asking if I was okay and I'd reply that I was totally fine and didn't care. That "I don't care" attitude seeped into every part of my life. When a "friend" introduced me to witchcraft and satanism, I thought . . . why not?

It all started innocently enough. I was just messing around with a Ouija board and asking the "spirits" things you shouldn't. But before I knew it, I was spiraling down a path toward full-blown devil worshipping. I began studying satanic rituals and occultist Aleister Crowley and how to make pacts with the devil. On weekends, I'd go to the local video store—the Pick A Flick—and rent my way through A to Z of demonic horror films. I would say terrible things in evil voices, at one point making a girl at my school burst into tears. I would take my Volkswagen Beetle to a Christian mechanic with the cassette tape player all set to blare satanic Grim Reaper songs as soon as they turned it on. It was a horrible phase that lasted about a year. My closest friends, part of our group we called the "Brew Crüe," began distancing themselves from me.

One night after partying, I crashed in the same room as my friend Ricky, lying on a couch in front of a bed, where he was with his girlfriend. As we were falling asleep, I started reenacting a scene from one of the movies I had watched, laughing maniacally like I was being possessed by a demon. I rolled over and suddenly all I saw was a watery red image and the face of a smiling demon calling me toward him with one long crooked finger and a twisted nail. There were no hallucinogens involved—we had just been drinking that night.

I was terrified and screamed as loud as I could. I hit the light, and Ricky and his girlfriend jumped up asking what had happened as they looked at me panting heavily and shaking uncontrollably. I told Ricky if I ever did that again, if I ever used that voice, or talked about devil worshipping, he had permission to hit me over the head with a bat. Ricky, who now seemed filled with a stoic calmness, full of the Holy Spirit, just looked at me and said simply, "I told you, didn't I?"

I didn't sleep a wink, and when the sun rose on that Sunday morning, I walked, still reeking of booze, and wearing the clothes from the night before, several miles to Edwards Road Baptist Church. I never looked back.

There was music, there was sport, and there was my faith. Those pillars from my youth laid a foundation and helped shape me into the man I am today, in ways big and small.

But in terms of some of the best interpersonal skills that I acquired growing up and could later use in my work undercover—there was no better training ground for me than the Silver Slipper.

The Silver Slipper was one of many "gentleman's clubs" (an oxymoron because gentlemen are hard to find) on Dorchester Blvd., which was just a stretch of road off I-26, which runs through South Carolina and dead-ends in Charleston. Locals had dubbed it "stripper's row." There were more than half a dozen clubs of varying degrees of seediness, including the Flying Dutchman, the Hayloft, and Miss Kitty's. The Silver Slipper was one of the more upscale clubs and a favorite for members of the Hell's Angels motorcycle club, and the navy and Marines from the nearby base.

When I was in college at Charleston Southern University, one of my buddies, Joe Pharis, was working as a bouncer at the Silver Slipper and helped me get a job. I had the physique to be a bouncer when I was in college and lifting like a beast.

But as I'd quickly discover, size didn't help you much when you had only two bouncers—sometimes even just one—for the entire bar, which could easily consist of a couple bachelor parties of ten to fifteen guys. It's not rocket science. It doesn't matter how tough you are when you're fighting fifteen guys at one time. I've been there in some knock-down-drag-outs when I was on the bottom of the pile hanging on for dear life and there's not much you can do.

That's where I learned the art of de-escalating—what some call "verbal judo."

Think of it like a baseball game—three strikes and you're out. Let's say some guy was getting a little "handsy" and starting to get drunk. I'd start interactions gently. Something like this:

"Hey buddy, are you having a good time?"

"Hell yeah, great time!"

"That's great, man, but you can't be grabbing the girls like that or my boss is going to want me to kick you out of here. Cool?"

"Yeah man, cool!"

Well, he's drunk so he keeps going. Strike one. I go back to remind him, still as my "buddy," and maybe this time I suggest he just sit on his hands for a bit. Strike two.

Some stop, but most don't, and there's strike three and you're out.

—

Even though I was bouncing, playing ball, and still partying a lot, I managed to come out of college on the Dean's List and a 3.8 GPA for my last two years.

Thanks to a criminal justice course I took as an elective, I changed my major to criminology, with a minor in psychology. By the time I graduated, I knew I wanted to go into law enforcement.

But it took awhile to get a job, as I was told by law enforcement agencies across South Carolina that they were not hiring white males at the time. After twelve months of applying to different agencies, I finally got a call to come to the Greenville County Sheriff's Office.

It was the fall of 1993, and at the age of twenty-two, I walked into the station in my suit and tie, introduced myself, and was taken to one of the top-floor offices with rows of cubicles and fluorescent lights.

As part of the application process, they gave me a piece of paper with all these crimes listed on it and asked me to fill it out. I had a clean record, but I was told to circle the crimes I'd committed, even if I was never caught.

Public indecency. *Yep.*
DUI. *Yep.*
Petit larceny. *Yep.*
Speeding. *Yep.*
Assault, malicious damage. *Yep and Yep.*

I handed the form back to a ranking deputy sheriff whose name I'll never forget although I'm sure he doesn't remember me: John Fouts.

John took the piece of paper, and an incredulous expression came across his face. "Scott, you've done all this?"

I nodded.

"But you never got caught?"

"No, sir."

He wanted to hear more.

The only excuse I really had was boredom. And there may have been some substances that aided in my decision-making. As for not getting caught? Maybe just street smarts and some dumb luck. Or maybe divine intervention. God had a different plan for me.

Indecency? Well, after a night of partying, and bored out of our minds, my buddies and I would go streaking. We'd strip down to our tennis shoes and stand by a stop sign on a busy street and strike a pose like statues. Just standing there, completely naked and still as traffic passed by. You should have seen the look on drivers' faces when they slammed on their brakes after processing the scene, and we took off running, giggling like little kids. It was comedy gold.

Stealing? Well, I wasn't into stealing, but as the big guy, I would block the view of the merchandise at a record shop or talk to the guy at the counter while my friends stole what they could.

Assaults and DUIs? I'm not proud of it, but I got into fights, and I've been too drunk to drive.

On I went, not holding back and telling John whatever he needed to know, but assuring him that was my past, and I had matured. All I wanted to be was a cop.

Only thing I can think of is that he appreciated my honesty, because I was allowed to continue through the process and was soon after hired. Who knows where my life would have taken me if I hadn't gone into policing?

Life is really about choices, and most of the time when you're choosing one thing, you're giving up another. I chose law and order.

2

THE BADGE

Greenville, South Carolina
1996

I was slouched down in the passenger's seat of a beat-up white Ford Econoline, wearing a stocking cap and bulky coat, trying to appear smaller than my 270-pound frame. In the driver's seat was one of Greenville, South Carolina's known drug users. He bore a resemblance to "Bubbles," the impossibly optimistic junkie from *The Wire*; slight, haggard-looking, with permanent dark circles under his eyes.

Bubbles was doing what he usually did—getting ready to buy crack cocaine. But on this day, he was working for us as a source, and we were prepping for what we call a "controlled buy."

Sources would agree to help law enforcement because they needed the money, or they wanted a deal to work off their own charge. Sometimes, they just wanted to do the right thing. We kept sources close, searching them and their vehicle before and after operations, and conducted surveillance of them to make sure they went in with only what we gave them for the "buy," and came back out with nothing but our evidence. It was important to document the chain of evidence and make sure whatever we did would stand up in court.

But it was always a stronger case if you had a cop-chaperone going undercover alongside them. And that was my role on that cold, gray, wet, and generally nasty afternoon.

I had joined the Greenville County Sheriff's Office in 1993, and spent the first three years on uniform patrol. Then I landed a coveted position and was promoted to investigator with the vice/narcotics squad. To say I was unprepared when I first joined the squad is an understatement.

On day one, my training officer asked me if I'd ever seen *Reservoir Dogs*. I hadn't, so that was my homework, to go home and watch it that night. The next day he said to me, "Now, that's a real undercover. That guy never broke role. He stayed undercover."

Well, as I got older and became more experienced, I realized that this was bad advice, a terrible example of what a "good" undercover agent is supposed to be. That guy—Mr. Orange—watched another cop get his ear cut off, set on fire, killed, and then *he* got shot, and he never broke role? No, thank you. There is no case worth that.

At the Sheriff's Office, we were fighting drugs at the local level, targeting mainly street dealers. Unlike my undercover work years later with the FBI, when our team could spend weeks, even months, building up my fake undercover profile before meeting a target, these cases were often impromptu.

For my first nighttime assignment I was told to just roll up at the appointed meet location, where I'd get wired up. Then I was instructed to drive down to a known drug trafficking area, roll down the window, and ask the dealer for a "twenty." None of the training officers seemed bothered by my size and that I wasn't exactly the picture of an emaciated crack user.

My heart was pounding, and butterflies were going mad in my stomach as I eased the car toward the dealers. It's almost comical to look back now and picture myself, shitting gold bricks, looking like a deer in the headlights, as I carefully stopped the car and waited for a dealer to run to me. I rolled down the window, just a crack, and carefully slipped out a twenty-dollar bill like I was inserting it into an ATM.

"What you want?"

"A twenty?" I said, in a high-pitched voice, as if it was a question.

He handed me a sliver, and I didn't have the experience yet to know if he was ripping me off. Nor would I have cared! I just wanted to get the hell out of there.

There were other skills I learned by being thrown into the deep end on the narcotics beat. Sometimes on the squad we'd target dealers growing pot in the mountains or running a remote drug operation. We'd get dropped by a Sheriff's Office helicopter at 3 a.m., then hike up another two miles to get in position for a surveillance operation. And wait.

I was so bored that I ate and drank everything I brought before the sun even came up. Unlike my fellow officers, who had a background in military, I wasn't accustomed to rationing the food or limiting my liquid intake so that I wasn't having to piss every half hour. That's what I like to refer to as self-correcting behavior. Funny now, not so funny then.

But it's amazing how quickly you can learn from your successes and failures. After about a year on the narcotics squad, I was pretty confident. I would report for duty, parking my candy-red Iroc-Z T-Top and walking into the station ready for whatever the shift would throw at me.

So I wasn't overly concerned sitting beside "Bubbles" as he eased his white van onto Cody Street. There was a hierarchy in the way drugs were dealt in the neighborhoods of Greenville. There was a street drug boss, who was the supervisor who ran each corner, intersection, or drug house. This guy—and it was always a guy—was the first line of defense, the one who gave the go-ahead for the deal if it looked safe, signaling to the low-level dealer (often a user) to go get the drugs. The merchandise was usually hidden somewhere nearby, behind a loose brick in a wall, in a hole, or buried in a bush. It was rare that anyone carried the drugs on their body. They were wary of the "jump out boys," as the dealers called us. Cody Street was a high-traffic, well-known dealing area.

But as we turned a corner, suddenly our target came into view. "Damn. You gotta be kidding me," I muttered under my breath. Then, as it always does when things get stressful, everything started to move in slow motion and there was only the soundtrack of my heart thumping in my ears.

I couldn't remember this dealer's name, but I definitely knew his face.

Just two weeks earlier, I had been helping our Southern Command Narcotics Squad execute a search warrant. As luck would have it, I was the investigator who had gotten *this* dealer out of bed and cuffed him. Later, back at the station, I had tried to build a bit of a rapport with him, talking in detail about our tattoos. Clearly, having all that police attention hadn't deterred him from getting right back out on the street.

I didn't let on to the source that I knew his target. I just looked the dealer dead in the eye as sweat started to drip under all my layers of clothing and my stomach knotted painfully. He returned my stare, not breaking eye contact as he slowly walked around the van, right up to my window to get a good look at me. In my hand, I was clutching the money for the deal.

"What's up?" I asked, watching his eyes finally leave my face to look at the cash. Then he looked to his guy who was slinging the drugs and said, "Go ahead." We did the deal.

When we later arrested him, he said, "I *knew* you were a cop."

I replied, "You *thought* I was a cop. But you had some doubt."

As it usually does in the world of criminals, greed won the day.

—

After my retirement from law enforcement in the summer of 2021, I was described in a *Rolling Stone* profile as a Hillbilly Donnie Brasco. I wear that title proudly and think the reputation of being able to relate to people, no matter their background or crime and whether I was in uniform on patrol or working undercover, began in those early policing days in Greenville.

I was a proactive officer right from the start, not the kind of deputy who would sit in a cul-de-sac, drinking coffee. If I wasn't responding to calls, I made it my mission to get to know the county, especially the rural roads of the Blue Ridge Mountains that extended all the way up to the border with North Carolina. We called that region "Northern Command Beat Area Number One." Since this was the mid-1990s, there was no such thing as Google Maps. You just had your *Rand McNally Road Atlas* and memory. And in that beat area, it was good to know the roads well. If you were dispatched to answer a call, you knew backup was at least thirty minutes behind you, and there was a good chance that by the time you arrived, whatever was happening would already be over.

In the mountains, I got to further practice my verbal judo, as talking was often your best weapon.

One day, I arrived on a call on a rural back road to find a woman holding her front tooth in her hand. I asked her partner what happened, and he said (and I'll never forget these words), "I told her if she didn't pass the salt, I'd knock her damn teeth out, and listen, Officer, well, she didn't pass the salt and I'm a man of my word."

I nodded, trying to give the impression I could relate. Then I asked him if he had heard of the O. J. Simpson case. Of course he knew it—everyone was obsessed with that story at the time. "Well, let me explain to you what has happened since the O. J. Simpson incident," I told him. "It's now a mandatory arrest if we witness any signs of physical altercation in a domestic dispute." I was trying to indicate that the situation was out of my hands—give him the impression that I wasn't any happier to arrest him than he was to be arrested.

Now it was his turn to nod. "Ah hell. It's okay," he said, "you're just doing your job," and he offered his wrists to be handcuffed.

On the forty-minute drive to the station, I asked what type of music he liked to listen to, and he said anything but that "rap crap." We put on a classic rock station, and Lynyrd Skynyrd took us the rest of the way down the mountain.

When I got to the Sheriff's Office sally port area to process him, it was hot, crowded, and noisy, but I could tell my fellow officers were paying us special attention, whispering a bit among themselves in a gossiping sort of way. I asked what was going on. "Do you know who he is?" one of the deputies asked me. "We don't go to his house without at least four of us. He fights all the time."

—

I had a lot of mentors inside the Sheriff's Office, but not all of the people I got valuable advice from were in law enforcement.

One lesson was pretty basic: If you're going undercover, make sure you look the part. My teachers for that were a charming, impeccably dressed, clean-cut gay couple that worked at "The Pantry"—a gas station and convenience store centrally located where three of my beat areas connected. I used The Pantry as my unofficial field office—drinking the fake cappuccino from their machine and using the spotless public washroom, which was always decorated with flowers, wallpaper, and some sweet-smelling potpourri. I'd also borrow their phone, since there weren't many cellphones back then, to make calls on follow-up investigations.

They never minded us being there. Having squad cars parked outside their store was a pretty good deterrent for any criminal activity. I was one of their regulars and they loved to tease me. Behind the counter they had tacked up a Polaroid photo of me, and underneath they'd written in black Sharpie: "Male chauvinist."

When I told the guys about my new position with the narcotics squad, they were very inquisitive about what I would be doing and the prospect of me trying to go undercover to buy cocaine on the club scene. They said my look screamed "cop," and mocked my high and tight haircut and insisted I get what was trendy at the time—shaved at the sides, mushroom side part on top. And they helped me with what I should wear, since all I owned were jeans and T-shirts. I got that haircut and purchased the clothing they suggested—Timberland boots and baggy corduroy pants. When I grabbed a pair of shades from their sunglasses selection on the counter, just to complete the look, they weren't impressed. "Those are *so yesterday*," I remember them saying, sighing, as I waited until they found the perfect pair. I started referring to them as my "fashion consultants." In the end I probably did more work on the street than in the clubs anyway. But when I did hang with the cocaine crowd as "Scott Anderson," it wasn't hard to blend in with my new look thanks to my fashion consultants.

I was happy for the two years I spent on the narcotics beat, but I knew my time working in Greenville was limited if I wanted to pursue undercover operations. There were only so many ways to change my hair, clothes, or backstory. I'd had more than just that one close call on Cody Street with Bubbles, when someone recognized me. One night up in the mountains I looked down the nose of a rifle as a dealer said, "My brother says you're a cop." His brother, of course, was right, and I had locked him up years earlier when I was in uniform.

It was really thanks to one of my sergeants on the narcotics squad that I started thinking about the FBI. Sergeant Mike Kellett was a former Marine, with a handlebar mustache, a stocky build, and Popeye forearms. One day when we were on surveillance Mike said to me, "You know, Kingpin [a nickname I got on the squad when I started making arrests] if I were your damn age, single, and I had a degree, man, I'd apply to the FBI."

So that's what I did.

—

It takes about a year to go through the FBI's application process. There are math tests, psychological and fitness assessments, and a bunch of interviews. Although I wore a suit, I showed up for one test with my beard and long hair, to a waiting room filled with clean-cut applicants; lawyers, accountants, and some members of the military wearing their dress uniforms. Although I had approval from the FBI applicant coordinator to maintain my appearance—needed at that time for the narcotics squad—it did not stop some very odd glances from my fellow applicants.

Part of the screening involved an incredibly lengthy and involved polygraph test that I think lasted at least three hours.

"Have you done any illegal narcotics within the last ten years?"

"No," I answered.

"Have you used marijuana in the last three years?"

I paused. "Is that a trick question?" I asked.

"No," the examiner answered.

Well, this was 1998, and I was a narcotics officer, and I sure as hell knew weed was illegal. But he replied that it would have been okay if I used it up to three years prior.

"Okay. My answer would still be no."

Then we went on to discuss the times I did use weed before going into law enforcement and the questions still continued: "Did you package it? Did you sell it?"

I said, "Look, I can answer all of your questions with this explanation." Then I described how as a teenager, I would go to parties with my friends, and we'd all add money to a pile. Someone would come back with weed, we'd smoke it, and if there was any left, someone would keep it. Only one time did I bring the leftovers with me, and I couldn't sleep, worried my mom would find it. I bet you I changed the hiding place five times that night. I never did that again. I think I was more scared of my mom than the police.

He persisted with the questions.

"How many times would you say you've used marijuana?"

"Ummmm . . . I'm not sure."

"Would you say no more than fifteen?"

So I replied, "Yeah . . . Sure . . . Fifteen sounds good," even though I had no idea what he meant by fifteen.

The agent did not like this casual answer and slammed the desk, screaming, pointing at me, "You think this is a joke?!?"

None of this made sense. I started to panic. We were talking about something from over a decade ago. And what did he mean by "fifteen"? Fifteen joints, fifteen times, fifteen pounds?

I had to guess that there was some elected official's kid, or someone with influence who wanted to become an FBI agent but had a recent weed habit (but no more than fifteen times), so they made this rule?

Anyway, I passed that test, because I got an FBI invitation letter to report to Quantico, Virginia, for training, on September 27, 1998.

At some point during our five months of training, we were asked to fill out a form that listed our preferences of the field offices where we wanted to be posted, rating them in order from 1 to 56. I sweated over that form, trying to figure out where I wanted to live, working my way up the East Coast so I could stay close to my family. I listed New York as number 36 out of the possible 56 field offices.

I got New York.

The problem was that the year I joined the FBI, Al Qaeda launched twin attacks on U.S. Embassies in Kenya and Tanzania, leaving 224 dead and thousands injured. Twelve Americans were among the dead. Resources had been poured into our Washington, DC, field office for the investigation, which meant management from the big offices—New York, L.A., Chicago, and San Francisco—were looking to fill vacancies.

I ended up loving my time in New York. I embraced the nightlife, explored the city, and spent a lot of time in Central Park. If anyone came to visit, I'd be the best tour guide, pointing out the restaurant that's in the openings for *Seinfeld* or the apartment building from *Friends*. I'd gotten to know the guards at the Empire State Building, so I could take my guests past the line and up a separate elevator to see the city at night.

But I knew it wasn't where I wanted to live for long. So when I got my first opportunity to go undercover out of state, even before I was officially trained and certified as an FBI undercover agent, I jumped at the chance. The way assignments worked back then is that headquarters would put out a call to undercover agents posted at all of the FBI's fifty-six field offices. The request could be specific, something like, "Looking for an Asian male, between 22–34 years old, proficient in Cantonese." If no one grabbed the assignment, then the net would be cast wider to those who weren't officially certified.

This request was to go undercover as a security guard, somewhere in Texas. I guess it was no surprise none of the certified agents jumped at the opportunity. The job didn't really sound like a sexy high-stakes scene from *Donnie Brasco*: cheesy polyester uniforms, a flashlight, and working third shift?

But I applied, happy to go undercover. New York had been great but I was struggling to afford to live and cursing a window air conditioner that barely provided any relief and the city's torturous street parking rules.

That case I worked in Texas remains classified to this day. It's too bad because there were damn good stories about that operation, and let's just say the target was, well, interesting.

What I can describe is the day-to-day drudgery of my cover. It was an exercise in patience. I had to pose as that security guard, working the night shift and living alone in a hotel room, for *a year*.

I was in Texas, near the end of that case, on the morning of September 11, 2001. I ended my shift like usual, around 7 a.m. Most mornings I'd go back to my hotel room, make a Jack and Coke (or two) and something to eat, watch a little TV, and then pass out until the afternoon. But I woke after only about an hour of sleep because my phone was vibrating like mad. I looked down and saw: missed call, missed call, missed call, missed call, missed call, missed call, missed call, and just as many voice messages.

I flipped the TV back on and watched the second plane hit New York's World Trade Center. I didn't go back to sleep and spent the rest of the day contacting my friends in New York and then reaching out to their families to let them know they were okay.

Of the 2,977 victims who died that day, 421 were emergency workers, the majority of whom were firefighters. Our Bureau lost FBI Special Agent Leonard W. Hatton after he helped evacuate people from the burning towers, just before they collapsed around him. Dozens of other agents have died in the years since of illnesses related to their investigation combing through the twisted metallic pile where the towers once stood, or other crash sites, or on Staten Island, where the toxic debris was taken. One of the victims was David LeValley, a friend and squad mate of mine.

Within a couple weeks of the attacks, as soon as the airspace opened up again, I was back in New York helping out, driving down the West Side Highway, which at the time was reserved only for emergency workers. It was lined with residents holding signs of support.

I was ready to stay—offering whatever help was needed.

But my transfer from New York to Texas, where I would officially be posted to our San Antonio Field Office, McAllen Resident Agency, had already been approved. My boss in New York knew how much I wanted to get out of the city and encouraged me to just go through with the transfer.

—

Once at the McAllen field office, I worked for about eight months with the drug squad, which was incredibly busy due to our proximity to the Mexican border.

Then in 2002, I got a slot at the FBI's Undercover School, and even though I knew I wanted this, I wasn't sure I was ready.

At the time, I wasn't physically doing well due to complications from back surgery. I had dropped about thirty pounds and spent three weeks of hell with damaged ligaments that made it feel as if I was drowning, gasping for air, when I tried to eat. Those three weeks, as I struggled to breathe, were some of the toughest and scariest of my life. I remember I pulled over to the side of road after getting the call to attend the FBI Undercover School and looked to God for some guidance. I didn't want to turn down the offer, but I also didn't want to fail. I asked him to let me know if I *wasn't* supposed to do this. No sign came.

As soon as I arrived back in Quantico, Virginia, on September 15, 2002, and started the FBI's certification school, I knew I had made the right decision, and this was where I wanted to be. It was an exhausting and grueling two weeks—no days off, very little, if any, sleep. On average, a little over half of those who get into this course make it through.

I sat in the front row and gazed up at one of my undercover heroes, Joe Pistone, a.k.a. Donnie Brasco. It was one of those theater classrooms, where the seats get higher with each row, and Joe had this habit of leaning forward when he talked, so he could see the students higher up. But he kept hitting my feet, despite my best efforts to move them out of his way. At one point he stopped and said, "Jesus, kid, either you got the biggest feet I've ever seen, or I just can't see." He threw down a few bucks and said, "Go get yourself a shine on me."

Once I'd made it through the program and was officially certified as an undercover agent, I went back to work in McAllen and started looking for undercover opportunities. Every two weeks I'd call the FBI Headquarters Undercover Unit, eager for work. "Hey, you got any roles for a redneck who doesn't speak any foreign languages?" Two weeks later: "Hey, you got anything . . ."

You get the picture.

While I didn't get a case quickly, that persistence did pay off, as I got a chance to go back to the Undercover School to be a role-player in scenarios and help with whatever else they needed. The problem was that this opportunity came at the exact same time I tried out to become a firearms instructor and was told by the San Antonio Field Office that I'd gotten a slot in the certification school during the same two weeks. The FBI firearms instructor certification course was grueling; if you failed to qualify on a firearms test, you were sent home. And people got sent home all the time. I didn't want to say no to either opportunity, so I ended up doing both. That meant I was at Quantico's Firearms Instructor School all day and role-playing at the Undercover School all night.

On the first evening, after I role-played in a scenario as a dirty banker, Steve Salmieri took me aside and told me he thought I "had something special." Salmieri was a close friend of Joe Pistone, and while maybe not as well known in public, he was an undercover legend. During his twenty-nine years at the FBI, Salmieri infiltrated the Mafia, biker gangs, and terrorist groups and ran the Undercover Unit at the FBI's headquarters.

I remember getting back to my dorm room at four or five in the morning, waking up my roommate, and telling him about the encounter. I was so pumped with adrenaline I barely slept for those fourteen days. When I look back now, I can see that Pistone, Salmieri, and some of the other OG FBI undercovers were passing the torch to the next generation.

3

OPERATION ROADKILL

Brockton, Massachusetts
July 29, 2005

The Foxy Lady Gentleman's Club in Brockton, Massachusetts, was pretty standard fare for a big strip joint. There were elevated stages beneath a tangle of spotlights hanging from the ceiling, and long, well-stocked bars that ran down the sides of the room. There was exposed wood, dark corners, naked women, and clothed men of all shapes and sizes. Cameras kept an eye on what the patrons were doing, along with the manager, who was a no-nonsense woman who seemed to know everyone and be everywhere.

It was about 9 p.m. on July 29, 2005, when my targets entered wearing their "colors"—black leather vests with cross pistons and a skull, who they'd nicknamed "Charlie." I was doing what I always did when at the Foxy Lady, just cracking jokes, working the room, sipping a couple Jack and Cokes, and maybe ordering a lap dance wearing an expression I had perfected of not looking too bored, or overly excited. She was doing her job; I was doing mine.

My targets were members of the Outlaws Motorcycle Club ("OMC"), one of America's most violent biker gangs and the historic archrival of the Hells Angels. "Outlaws Forever. Forever Outlaws," they liked to say.

The Outlaws, like the Hells Angels, the Bandidos, the Pagans, the Mongols, and other outlaw motorcycle clubs, called themselves the "one percenters," meaning they considered themselves hardcore bikers on the fringes of society. The term goes back to 1960, when William Berry, who was the president of the American Motorcyclist Association (AMA) at the time, said that 99 percent of motorcyclists were law-abiding citizens.

I had been building my cover for weeks before coming here—making sure I had a solid, plausible backstory that would not raise any suspicions when I tried to infiltrate the group. At the FBI, we called it creating "a legend," and it meant I had to memorize everything about my fake identity, right down to the name of my favorite childhood pet. I stayed close to my real identity, just to make it both believable and easy to remember.

I became Scott Callaway, a Harley-loving, whiskey-drinking, site-survey specialist from Texas, which explained why I traveled a lot and what a Southerner might be doing in a Massachusetts bar.

We already had some intel on the local chapters of the Outlaws, so when Spanky walked into the Foxy Lady, I ID'd him right away. About five-foot-ten, flattop, goatee, and all tatted up, I knew Spanky was a longtime member of the Taunton, Massachusetts, Outlaws chapter, and that he loved attention and liked to surround himself with big guys. What I *hadn't* expected was that he would come in with half a dozen other members with their Outlaw colors blazing. The intel from the case team was that they would *not* wear their colors in a place like the Foxy Lady.

Well shit, that changes things, I thought. *Now what am I going to do? I can't go up and say casually, "Do you boys ride?"*

I had to make sure I didn't appear too eager to engage them, so I just continued being me and ordering drinks. My Southern accent was helping me meet people because every time I asked for a whiskey, I got a lot of "Where the hell are you from?" As our group got bigger, the conversation and laughing got louder; loud enough to reach the other end of the bar and get Spanky's attention. He couldn't help but wonder who this six-foot-four guy with the big laugh and weird accent was.

"Where the fuck are you from?" he shouted across the bar.

I looked around, innocently, with my best *who me?* face.

"Well, I'm from deep South Texas," I replied.

Spanky had read the news apparently, as he asked, "Isn't it flooding down there right now?"

"Hell yeah. I made sure I tied off my trailer so it wouldn't float away before coming here."

The small talk continued.

"How tall are you?"

I called back, "About five-foot-nine."

Soon after, he sent me over a drink.

I went to the bathroom alone about thirty minutes later, encouraged by the scene so far. But as I stood before the urinal, the door swung open. Without turning around, I looked at the Plexiglas ad framed on the wall in front of me and studied the reflection of the guy who'd just entered. I didn't know who he was but had observed that he was with Spanky and the others, and he wasn't wearing the OMC colors. He was dressed in jeans and a gray T-shirt with black trim, so I could see his muscular build and the sleeve of tattoos on his left arm. In his left ear he had three stainless-steel ball hoop earrings.

He looked left. He looked right. He looked under the stall doors. Then he turned toward me and walked slowly. I braced, getting ready to be jumped.

But instead, he just came up beside me: "What brings you to Massachusetts?"

It was the start of a beautiful friendship.

—

The FBI would dub this Outlaws case "Operation Roadkill." It was not my first undercover operation after being officially certified as an undercover agent. I also had cameos on other cases, which are basically defined the same way a "cameo" is in acting—a smaller part, or a walk-on role, to support the main characters.

In one case, I was hanging out with a source in Oklahoma, trying to ingratiate myself in an illegal chop shop business and purchase stolen vehicles. At the time, FBI agent Barry Loggins, who was known as Bo, was a mentor and friend of mine, with a ton of experience in the undercover program. In a strange coincidence of timing, I was returning a covert vehicle for the Oklahoma case one day when Bo came out of his office and told me he had just hung up the phone with the Boston Field Office undercover coordinator. And he had been asking about me.

"He pinned me in a corner and asked me if I would personally vouch for you," Bo told me. "And I said yes." Then he paused. "So don't fuck this up."

"Absolutely, sir," I replied. "No pressure."

It was an amazing opportunity. I'd already been to Boston to interview for the Outlaws case, but I think it was Bo's blessing that sealed the deal. And I landed that case at a great time in my life. I loved living in Texas, and soon after moving there from New York and buying a house I married the love of my life, Kara.

—

I'd first met Kara through my friend Brian Cox when I was living in Greenville, South Carolina. Brian came from a family of NYPD officers, but we knew each other from our days as bouncers at the Silver Slipper.

Brian had saved me more than once over the years, including giving me his couch when a roommate I had planned to live with suddenly got evicted and I was stuck with all my worldly possessions in my car, and too stubborn to move back home. During that time—before I found law enforcement—Brian helped me set up my first bank account and save my wages to eventually get my own place. His future wife, Andrea, was friends with Kara and keen to set us up. The problem was that Kara and I lived fourteen hundred miles away from each other.

These days, it's not unusual to meet your partner online, or get to know someone intimately by text or phone before meeting in person, but in the mid-1990s, that still seemed rare. But once I got up the courage to call her, we talked every night, night after night, for months. Then I finally saved up enough money to visit, and on what would be only the second flight I had ever taken in my life, booked a nine-day trip to meet her in Nebraska. It was a gamble—nine days is a long time if it's not going well.

If you ask Kara, the moment she knew we would be together happened on one of those nights. We were both in her little rental home getting ready to go out. Kara was blow-drying her hair and I was waiting on the couch when I saw her dad's acoustic guitar. After tuning it up a little, I started playing a Zakk Wylde song. Kara came out and just stared, wondering how the hell I knew she was a rabid fan of the long-haired lead guitarist for Ozzy Osbourne.

It would be a few years later, and a lot of long-distance dating, before we were married in December 2001 and moved into our first home, in McAllen, Texas. By the time I started on the Outlaws case in the summer of 2005, we had two daughters, aged three and one. Life was pretty sweet.

But what I didn't know then was that this case was about to push me to the limit. I'd come close to losing my marriage, my sanity, and my life.

—

The big guy who came into the bathroom at the Foxy Lady to check me out was named Scott Towne.

"Scott T," as he was known, was a mixed martial arts underground fighter. While he wasn't an official, patch-carrying member of the OMC, he was widely respected and feared in the group. I was relieved my cover story hadn't strayed too far from the truth, because Scott T's questions that first day were probing, and there were a few uncomfortable coincidences. For instance, when I said I was living in McAllen, Texas, he replied that he had been there a few times and started rattling off neighborhoods and streets. He also knew a lot about Greenville, South Carolina, where I was born.

I liked Scott T right from the beginning and we hit it off immediately. We were so similar. We liked all the same things, carried ourselves the same way, had the same sense of humor. I couldn't help but think again about that proverbial fork in the road, when I went the law-and-order way. If I hadn't, maybe I would have become Scott T.

Over the weeks and months that followed, he opened up to me, telling me details about both his "professional" and personal life. Before he started doing business with the Outlaws, he had made money fighting pit bulls all across America. That's how he knew Texas and South Carolina and a bunch of other states. He'd never been arrested for it but had some close calls, including one in Austin, Texas, he told me, where he was running dogs alongside a crooked cop. Another law enforcement unit raided one of their fights, and he managed to escape with his dog. The cop wasn't so lucky.

Scott T taught me a lot about the Outlaws and how they operated, despite his status of not being a "patch-carrying member." He said he could join pretty much whenever he wanted but was worried about being targeted and going to jail. The story he told me was that years ago he'd had a close call with law enforcement and had to pay an attorney a huge sum of money to get out of it. It scared him. He had four daughters and didn't want to leave them.

He also wasn't really impressed with some of the Taunton chapter members, thinking they were a little weak, and hadn't been in any fights to prove their worth. He may have been scared of going to jail, but Scott T didn't back down from a fight. He proudly told stories of past "beatdowns" he'd done on behalf of the Outlaws in Ohio and elsewhere, and how the Hells Angels feared him because he'd once nearly killed one of their members.

And he had seen some action. An OMC brother died in his arms, he claimed, from a bullet that was meant for him.

Scott T's homelife definitely didn't sound like a pretty scene. He claimed his biological father, who was unknown to him until he was thirty-five years old, had ties to the Genovese crime family in New York. He once put a gun to his own mother's head and almost killed her, he told me. After that, he said he quit drinking alcohol. (Although he would go out to drink with me all the time.)

Some of these stories, we couldn't verify. Our team was busy trying to build a case with evidence about current criminal activities, and I never wanted to look like I was interrogating him. But I never thought Scott T was just a big talker. One time when I was at his place at about three-thirty in the morning, he took me to a back bedroom, pulled out a white plastic bag, and proudly displayed a black vest bearing the Hells Angels colors. It was a souvenir from his beatdown, he said, and he'd wear the vest when engaged in criminal activity so the victim and authorities would think he was with the Hells Angels, not the Outlaws.

Sometimes in long-term undercover operations there's that one guy—the one you get really close to and know he's got your back, and he believes you have his. For Operation Roadkill, that guy was Scott T.

But I've never really had a bond like that with a target. Ever. Before that case, or after.

—

The 11th Annual Outlaws Motorcycle Club Lobster Festival was held on August 13 in Brockton, Massachusetts, and I had a personal invite from Spanky.

Before he left the Foxy Lady that first night we met, he had given me two of his business cards, one for a twenty-four-hour towing company and the other for a tattoo parlor. There were four different numbers listed, and Spanky told me that whenever I was in town, I could reach him at any of those. Earlier in the evening we had been talking about riding and I let him know my motorcycle was back in Texas. "Don't worry," he said. "If you need one, I'll get you a scooter to ride." Then he told me about the Lobster Festival. "All you need to say to get in," he said, "is Spanky sent me."

But on that day, I didn't go alone. I had arranged to arrive with Scott T and I trailed him like a devoted puppy. Whenever anyone asked me who I was, I'd say, "I guess I'm his bitch today."

These outlaw motorcycle biker parties are pretty public affairs, with hundreds of guests spilling in and out of the clubhouse. This one was held at the Brockton chapter, and while you needed an invite to get in, there were dozens of cops in unmarked units on the perimeter, filming and taking photos. My own team was out there, and I'd occasionally get a glimpse of one of them.

When we walked in, I bought a handful of "Brockton bucks," which could be used for drinks and lobsters, and purchased a few raffle tickets. There was live music, and there were women and tons of motorcycles, all swirling in a sea of black leather.

Thanks to my new friend Scott T, over the next four and a half hours, I met many members of the Outlaws from the northeast region, including those at the Taunton and Brockton chapters, like "Handsome Gary," "Antichrist," "Monster," and "Fordy." As we were getting ready to leave, the crowd quieted for a moment for the raffle draw.

"Dude," I said to Scott T when the number was called, "I think I won."

I stared at the ticket in my hand in disbelief. All afternoon I was carefully navigating the crowd, walking that tightrope of attracting attention, but not too much attention. And now I'm being called up on stage in front of hundreds because I won the damn raffle? I tried to get Scott T to go up for me, but he wouldn't do it.

I made my way through the crowd, handed in my winning ticket, collected the wad of cash as quickly as I could, and then went to the clubhouse bar and bought two Jack and Cokes and put in the jar the largest tip I've ever left in my life.

—

The Lobster Festival afterparty was back at the Foxy Lady. There were many Outlaws who came, including Spanky, and a member from the Maine chapter who said he had just gotten out of jail two hours earlier. Scott T was there, too. I knew I was being constantly observed, and my mind was always racing, but so far, I was passing all of their unofficial tests. Part of the reason Spanky was so friendly with me was that he saw an opportunity. The Outlaws wanted to start a Cape Cod chapter and were looking at me and Scott T as the inaugural members. Cape Cod was Hells Angels' territory, so they knew they needed some big dogs who could handle themselves and establish territory in case there were turf wars.

The Foxy Lady on a Saturday night was packed. Our group filled one back part of the bar, and we were pretty much minding our own business. Unfortunately, it didn't last long.

With all due respect to New Jersey, the best way I can describe the group of guys that suddenly were in my face is to say they were "Jersey Shore"—tight shirts, lots of gel, and spray tans. I did my best to defuse the situation, leaning on the skills from my bouncing days, when I'd be faced with someone all hyped on that toxic combination of testosterone and booze, which I like to call "liquid stupidity." I just kept talking to the lead guy, trying to boost his ego and reassure him the Outlaws didn't want to mess around with guys like him. Stuff like "You're good, buddy." "Nobody wants to fight you." "Everybody's just having a good time." Finally, he did walk away.

But just as soon as he was down, his stocky friend was up and on me, yelling and shit-talking. I was wearing a "Support Your Local Outlaws" shirt that I'd been given at the Lobster Festival, and behind me was a semicircle of leather. I knew they were all watching and that I was once again being pushed out on a tightrope, trying to talk my way out of this but also aware I couldn't look weak. I "politely" told him to sit down.

That's when the first punch came. I actually managed to dodge several, but there was a bench right behind me, and when I bumped into it, my knees buckled, and I ended up in a seated position. Then came the hit. *Pow.* Jersey Shore landed one right on my cheek. I dodged again, but his fist found my other cheek. *Pow.* By the third punch, I knew I could justify taking action as this would qualify as self-defense, not to mention I'd lose any respect I had gained from the Outlaws if I just sat there, taking it. I fought back. Quick elbows to the head. I grabbed him and we knocked a table over. Falling to the ground, I applied a carotid restraint, better known as a blood choke.

That's when I heard, "Brockton Police. Don't move!"

My heart sank, knowing how complicated the case would now get if I got arrested. I let go and stood up.

Suddenly everyone in the bar was talking to the cops—taking my side.

It wasn't him.

He tried to talk him down.

Spanky spoke up. "He told him to stop forty times." It wasn't forty times, but I appreciated the help. The cops didn't even come to talk to me, just handcuffed the other guy and took him outside.

Later that night, Spanky talked about the fight as if we'd just returned home from war. "This is my guy, this is my guy," he told the other members, slapping my back. "We've shed blood together. We fucking bled together." I thought to myself, *We?* But I looked at him sincerely and once again knew I should stroke the ego. "Yeah, man," I replied. "I appreciate you having my back."

The next day I boarded a plane home to McAllen, Texas. Touching down on the tarmac, I took a deep breath and readied myself to return once again to being Scott Payne.

4

RUNNING ON EMPTY

Taunton, Massachusetts
July 2005–October 2006

I was constantly on the move, running myself down, physically and mentally. Being an undercover agent on Operation Roadkill was not my only FBI obligation. People picture our role in cases like these through a Hollywood lens, where an agent fully embodies the fake identity in the most extreme method-actor fashion you can imagine. We go underground for months, or even years. The truth is, during my time in the Bureau, being a full-time undercover agent was pretty rare.

While I worked Operation Roadkill, I was also still the primary undercover agent for the Oklahoma case, which had morphed into a public corruption investigation because someone from the local law enforcement had a hand in the illegal chop shop. That meant some weekends I was still calling Spanky, Scott T, and the guys in Massachusetts to keep the case moving, and collecting evidence, even when I was with the Oklahoma crew at their "Redneck Yacht Club," the party barge where we drank on the decks of their tied-off houseboats and ski boats.

I was also still a case agent generating and running long-term investigations. That meant I would have to develop sources and be in charge of other investigations whenever I was back in McAllen. Here's one example of an investigation I oversaw during those years. It started with a call from an inmate at the Federal Detention Center in Houston. This guy was a member of the Almighty Latin King Nation, a powerful prison and street gang, and was near the end of his sentence. He contacted us because another inmate, Joel Lopez Sr., had tried to hire him to kill a United States district court judge and a woman who he claimed owed him $100,000 in a drug debt. Lopez had been sentenced to life for drug crimes by this federal judge, and in his twisted logic, he thought if the judge was dead, it would *help* in his appeal. He was willing to pay our source $3 million to kill the two of them and gave him his wife's number, telling him to contact her once he was released. When he contacted Lopez's wife on a burner phone we gave him, she responded: "I've been waiting for your call." The investigation culminated with a sting operation with our source as he pretended to go forward with the murders.

Mr. Lopez, aged fifty-one, was given another life sentence for his "murder-for-hire" attempt.[1]

In addition to all these roles, I was also the "principal relief supervisor." In other words, I would run the squad when the boss was away. It was not out of the ordinary to have to juggle multiple cartel kidnapping and extortion cases. One week, there were four at the same time.

Lastly, I was on the SWAT team and the lead tactical and firearms instructor for the FBI's McAllen field office at the time, which meant some weeks when I'd be home in Texas, I'd be on the range teaching agents to shoot in a climate with a heat index of 120 and the humidity 90 percent or more. I'd drink a gallon of water and a gallon of Gatorade and still not piss all day.

I thought I was managing pretty well. It would take a few years for me to realize the actual toll it was having on me, and how the relationships I held dear were suffering.

At home, I was basically a ghost. Even when I was there, I wasn't. I'd come back from a trip to Massachusetts, and Kara, excited to have me home, would happily declare she'd secured a babysitter for the night and we could enjoy a nice dinner out. I'd try to look enthusiastic, but all I wanted was to be at home with a meal that wasn't from a drive-through or restaurant. I didn't care, I could have had Hamburger Helper and been happy.

When we did stay home, I wasn't offering much. I'd pour some Jack and Coke and cradle my eldest girl, who was three years old at the time, in the rocking chair, playing with her hair, and trace my finger along her tiny face. I'd hum her either Elvis's "Are You Lonesome Tonight?" or "An American Trilogy." When she was asleep, I'd do the same bedtime routine with my one-year-old daughter. By the time I'd crawl into bed with Kara, I was half-asleep before my head even hit the pillow.

—

After that Lobster Festival and impressing Spanky with how well I handled the fight at the Foxy Lady, I started getting more invites to Outlaws get-togethers. The following month, in September 2005, I went to the Chili Chowder Festival, in Bridgewater, Massachusetts, where I got a chance to talk to Joseph Noe, a.k.a. "Joe Doggs," the Taunton chapter president.

Joe Doggs had spiky blond hair and a goatee and was only about five-ten, with a medium build—unless he was taking prednisone for his asthma, in which case his face and body would blow up like a puffer fish. When I met him that September afternoon, he was already high, twitchy, nervous, and sniffing like crazy. I assumed it was cocaine, but he could have been hyped up on anything.

I also met Brian Delavega, a.k.a. "Clothesline," for the first time that day. Clothesline didn't say much and wasn't as big as some of the other guys, but I knew he was the group's enforcer. He was clean-shaven, with intense eyes, short hair, and muttonchops tattooed along his jawline. Across his neck he'd inked the words "Live free or die." I remember when I offered Clothesline a Jack and Coke he said, "I'm allergic to Jack Daniel's. Every time I drink it, I break out in cuffs." That's funny!

I tried to remember all these details and the names of the other members I met—there was Dozer, Willie, Bear, Charbo, and about a dozen others. I'd repeat their nicknames, trying to keep everyone straight for the end-of-day reports we called "302s." I didn't start equipping myself with audio and video recording equipment until I was about three months into the case, had gained their trust, and no longer worried they might search me. Those recordings would be incredibly helpful for my note-taking, and part of the evidence we would need in court. But for those first few months, all I had was my memory. Luckily, I had been blessed with a good one.

Once again, law enforcement was all over the biker gathering (the Chili Chowder Festival), with uniformed state troopers walking boldly through the crowd. Several members of the Outlaws expressed their total disgust to me. Spanky was also getting a little paranoid about the "Feds" watching and listening to us and advised that we be careful whenever talking by phone. Back then, most of the guys used push-to-talk Nextels, which were basically chunky walkie-talkies. The key business was done in person, and fully patched members also met once a week in the clubhouse to discuss business at what they called "church." A lot of church had to do with club business, like the paying of chapter dues. Even though they weren't much, the club didn't mess around with their membership fees. One of the members, "Chocolate Scott," used to say, "I don't care if you've got to knock off an old lady on the way here, you show up with your money."

We left the festival in small groups and staggered our departures to try to avoid being harassed as a group by law enforcement. It didn't matter, though; I still got stopped by the state troopers as I left with Scott T and a couple others. Of course, they had no idea I was an FBI agent.

"Do you know your plates are expired?" the trooper asked me.

I answered honestly, "No."

"Well, they are."

I replied, "I guess you'll have to take that up with Avis, because I rented this thing."

I actually wasn't trying to be a smart-ass, but Scott T loved it, later relaying the story to the other guys at the bar. The troopers also questioned me about what I was doing in Massachusetts and why I had an Outlaws supporter shirt. "They're my friends," I answered.

And by then, they were.

—

Early in January 2006, while back at home in McAllen with Kara and our two daughters, I sent Scott T and Joe Doggs a text.

"Long time no talk 2. I got hitched!!? What's up?"

I had to get "married" out of necessity. Although I liked my cover to be as close to my real life as possible, it made sense when I started this case to say I was single. (Although do you know how hard is to get rid of the ring impression and tan line?) As a single guy, I figured, I could dodge some personal questions about my homelife, and I wouldn't have to think about possibly bringing in a female undercover agent to pose as my wife.

But that became a problem. By this point, I was five months into the case, and it was getting harder to deflect offers to hook up with the "sheep." That's what the women who hang around were known as in the one percenter biker world. The women were often addicted to drugs, and the guys did with them what they wanted. If it turned into more than just sex, then a "sheep" was "claimed," and she would wear a patch on her jacket that read: "Property of . . ." After that, the woman was the member's old lady and off-limits.

Being married, of course, didn't totally insulate me from this scene. Most of the members were still married and had women on the side. But after I "got married," I relayed to them a story about being cheated on once, and how it damn near killed me. I didn't want to do that to anybody, I'd tell them. "You do you, and I'll do me."

Scott T and Joe Doggs were shocked by the out-of-the-blue marriage, but more interested in getting me back to Massachusetts.

"Damn Tex . . . when you coming up . . . congrats on the new start . . . best of luck . . . let's get things in motion we are losing money," wrote Joe Doggs.

I wrote back: "Thanks bro! I'll be there in a couple of weeks. We'll talk."

"Cool dog . . . tell the mrs I said im sorry 4 her . . . call me b4 u hit the air."

Some one percenter bikers did have day jobs, but at the Taunton chapter only two members did. One was a tattoo artist and a piercer, and another member who ran a towing company, which was on the business card Spanky gave me that first day we hung out. The rest, including Joe Doggs, really needed some cash, so it was the perfect time for me to start building out my legend as a high-ranking member of an international theft ring. I wasn't just a site surveyor, I'd eventually let them know I also moved stolen goods south of the border for cash.

Probably the most important aspect of building an undercover investigation is that once you've ingratiated yourself—"ingratiated" is a word we used a lot in the FBI undercover community—you have to let your targets initiate the criminal activity. We already had what we called "predication," meaning that thanks to the work of the case team for more than a year before I joined, we knew many of the targets were already engaged in criminal activity. And I was lucky that it didn't take long for Joe Doggs and the others to start talking dirty to me, bragging about past exploits or their criminal ambitions. But talking about it isn't enough to take someone to jail. So that's kind of the art of what undercover agents do in gathering the evidence we need.

Joe Doggs was especially keen on drugs, and he figured since I lived on the border with Mexico, I had easy access. But I made drugs my red line at first—insisting I didn't transport them because it was too risky with the alphabet boys. That's what criminals called the enforcement agencies: FBI, the DEA (Drug Enforcement Administration), ATF (Alcohol, Tobacco, Firearms and Explosives), and ICE (Immigration and Customs Enforcement).

Once he found out I moved stolen goods, Joe Doggs asked what sold well south of the border. I told him Harleys and V8 4X4s were in high demand. I was just telling them what was true, and let their minds do the rest.

To help build my bona fides for this theft ring I was supposedly a part of, I flew back to Massachusetts at the end of January, having already dropped some hints with Joe Doggs that one of my truckers might be going through town. Maybe he would want to come with me to see how it all worked?

"If it puts money in my pockets, I'll do anything," Joe Doggs replied.

One chilly evening just after midnight, I drove my rented SUV with Joe Doggs in it along Highway 24 South to our meeting spot—a pretty desolate exit with a gas station and Burger King.

We parked, and before getting out, I slowly counted out a wad of cash and placed it in a Burger King paper bag, making sure Joe Doggs was watching my every move. Then I introduced Joe Doggs to my "trucker," who I'll call Johnny (another FBI undercover agent doing a cameo appearance on the case), and started to inspect the shipment of "stolen" power tools, which were boxed and packed tightly in the truck trailer. I took one of the power tools from the pile and gave it to Joe Doggs as a little token of my appreciation. I gave Johnny the bag of cash.

On the drive back to the Foxy Lady, Joe Doggs seemed convinced I was the real deal.

"That's a little score for you, huh? A couple hundred dollars?"

"More than that."

"All I saw was some power tools," he said.

"Exactly," I replied, smiling, letting his imagination take him the rest of the way.

By the spring of 2006, Operation Roadkill was picking up speed fast. After our dog and pony show with "Johnny," Joe Doggs offered me three Harleys, which would be reported stolen for the insurance. One of the Harleys belonged to Clothesline and one to a member known as "Rain." I can't remember where the third one came from. The way the plan worked was that I'd pay him a hot (stolen) rate for the bikes and then "transport" them to Mexico for profit.

But it didn't take long for them to move on from insurance scams to greater criminal offenses like stealing cars and pickup trucks. One truck they even got by carjacking at gunpoint someone who owed them money. We also learned of extortions and, of course, their continued drug trafficking. The case was really starting to take shape.

Scott T started talking more and more about transporting weapons as well, saying he had access to anything I wanted, including rocket-propelled grenades (RPGs), bazookas, and grenades. But they always circled back to drugs, which I steered them away from for various reasons, including the fact that the FBI couldn't give the Outlaws cocaine to deal on the streets of America.

Meanwhile, the biker war between the Outlaws and the Hells Angels was heating up dangerously.

On April 2, on the busy I-95 of West Haven, Connecticut, Hells Angels leader Roger "Bear" Mariani was gunned down in the middle of the afternoon as he rode with more than two dozen others. The shooter was one of four men riding in a green truck with Florida license plates.[2]

I was back in McAllen when I heard about the killing, and my mind immediately returned to a call a day or so earlier with Scott T. Every call or conversation was logged and recorded, but at the time, that one didn't seem particularly important. It was just Scott T telling me about how he had been partying with Clothesline and some out-of-state Outlaws he identified only as "Dano" and "Minus." But guess where they were from? That's right, visiting the northeast from *Florida*.

The Outlaws' regional boss, Marty Warren, had warned all members to lay low for a while and not wear their colors. I remember one night around this time when I was back in Massachusetts and we were drinking at the Foxy Lady, and Clothesline told me he wasn't scared. "I knew when I signed up, I could end up dead, end up in jail, shot, or in a gutter," he said. That was the same night Clothesline had sat down near me to get a massage from one of the dancers, when suddenly there was a huge *thump.* I jerked my head to look down at Clothesline's feet.

"Oh shit," he muttered and quickly reached down to retrieve his pistol that had just landed, in full public view.

He jammed the gun into his pocket as he watched me and the other guys looking at him.

"What?" I smirked, looking around. "Nobody's ever seen a paperweight?"

Later that night he confided in me what I already suspected—that he had been nervous when I went off alone with Joe Doggs to meet my "trucker," Johnny. I told him I respected that. He was doing his job.

But I knew also Clothesline was starting to unravel, drinking heavily, doing a lot of cocaine, and bringing that gun everywhere he went. He talked about outrageous plots, telling me that he wanted to use a Bobcat tractor and crash through a wall of a nearby gun shop so he could steal a cache of weapons. He seemed reckless, so it didn't come as a surprise that a couple months later he was arrested by the local cops for an attempted breaking and entering and spent some weeks in jail.

It wasn't just Clothesline who was on edge as the violence was escalating. One night, a bar crawl took us from the clubhouse to Lombardi's Bar, then another place called Christopher's Bar, until finally ending up at the Foxy Lady. Just as the club was closing, the brother of a former Outlaws member, who was extremely inebriated, started trash-talking Joe Doggs and Scott T.

I was paying the bartender at the time, and when I looked back up Joe Doggs and Scott T were gone. My Spidey senses went into overdrive and I got a bad feeling as I walked out of the club. Sure enough, in the parking lot Joe Doggs and Scott T were beating the shit out of that drunk guy as his four friends were dipping in and out of the action. I had no choice but to jump in and started tossing guys, shouting "back the fuck up!" I was making it appear like I was in the fight, but really what I was doing was trying to break it up and de-escalate; trying to help these guys before they got killed.

The drunk guy, bleeding profusely, started to walk away as if he was throwing in the towel, muttering, "I'm sorry, Joey, I'm sorry. I'm sorry." And then in a drunken sudden move, he turned back around and started trash-talking again. "I'm going to tell my brother and he's going to beat the shit out of you . . ."

For whatever reason, he then decided to charge right at me. He swung. I blocked him. And down we went as I held him in a rear choke hold. Seeing the blood spurt from his head, I picked him back up and said something like, "This guy can't even hold his own fucking blood," as I led him toward his car.

My cover team, as usual, wasn't far away. They were watching from a nearby parking lot, and I knew if we went much longer, they'd have to step in. We couldn't let someone get seriously injured or die on our watch.

Thankfully, the drunk guy finally left with his friends, and everyone cooled down. Our surveillance followed their vehicle until they were far enough out of the area and then got a local marked police unit to stop them to make sure they were okay. We call this a "wall off," which means the law enforcement action is far enough away from the incident it doesn't seem suspicious. The local cop would see the severely injured passenger and call an ambulance.

Drunk guy *and* Operation Roadkill would live another day.

The annual Sturgis Motorcycle Rally bills itself as "The Ride. The Roar. The Rally." Hundreds of thousands of biker enthusiasts take over the town of Sturgis, South Dakota, every year for ten days and ten nights. The Hells Angels have a clubhouse right on the main strip, but this is a decades-old bike rally that attracts people from all over the world. There are vendors and concerts, and camping and bars and buffalo burgers. It's a pretty wicked time.

To meet with our local FBI team and prep for the next week I arrived early, on August 11, 2006, just before Joe Doggs and the rest of the Taunton chapter members of the Outlaws were supposed to get there. I was standing in the FBI office when word came of a shooting. Five people had been shot—three Outlaws members—Thomas Haas, Allen Matthews, and Danny Neace—and two women, Claudia Wables and Susan Evans-Martin, who were with them.[3]

"Okay, get on out there," someone from my case team said, almost casually. My mind was moving quickly. If this was a hit by the rival Hells Angels—which would soon be confirmed—it would be an escalation of what was already a heated battle. Was this retaliation for "Bear"? We weren't sure, but it seemed more than coincidental. I had no desire to jump into the middle of it.

There happened to be a seasoned and well-respected undercover agent in the office that day—not on my case, but he was just there and listening to our discussion. He stepped between me and the team and said, "I don't think that's a good idea."

Now, I can't say I was hiding behind him, because although he was a stocky, well-built guy, he was quite a bit shorter. But I remember the relief as I stood there nodding, and thinking, *Yeah. Tell them why. I got enough holes in my body!*

I was just so exhausted by this point. No days off for weeks. I had jumped on a plane to Sturgis directly from teaching at the grueling two-week FBI Undercover School in an undisclosed location in the south. When I got to Sturgis, I had given the South Dakota team anything that identified me as "Scott Payne," and quickly resumed the role of "Scott Callaway." Now this?

Eventually we decided the trip was a bust. Aside from the danger of being caught in the crossfire, everyone would be laying low, so it wasn't a great time to collect intelligence. There was another undercover agent with me, who had been posing as one of my truckers. We walked around the Outlaws campsite for about half an hour, saying some hellos, and just being seen.

I handed in my recording equipment and jumped on my bike.

It was a perfect summer night as I rode down Keystone's main street, which almost looked like a set for an old Western. I was on my way to Mount Rushmore, which I'd never seen, taking in deep breaths of the fresh air and a big night sky of stars. There was just the sound of my rumbling Harley and the feeling of a warm breeze. For these precious minutes, I didn't have to work. I could just experience the moment.

I parked and walked out to gaze up at the faces of George Washington, Thomas Jefferson, Theodore Roosevelt, and Abraham Lincoln rising up from the dense green tree line. As I stood there, a spectacular fireworks show erupted.

Here I was, this South Carolina boy seeing in person something I'd only ever seen on TV, back in the days when there were only three television stations. At the end of the night, the national anthem would play as images of an American flag, an eagle, and Mount Rushmore filled the screen before it was just those colored bars and white noise.

I stood there and felt a rare moment of peace and patriotism.

—

The fight was about our youngest daughter.

Things got really tough with Kara after Sturgis. I had come back home to have surgery on my torn rotator cuff, and my phone wouldn't stop ringing. My case team was leaving message after message, *when can you do this, when can you do that?* Meanwhile, I was also getting calls from Scott T and the boys, concerned about how my surgery had gone and wishing me a speedy recovery. When I finally called an impatient member of my case team back, I explained, "I've been on a fentanyl patch for seventy-two hours. Hell, I can't even finish peeing before I need to sit down."

Even though I knew it was a slippery slope, and the bad guys weren't my friends, I couldn't help but think about how I was being treated better by hardcore criminals than some members of my team.

But not wanting to let anybody down, I quickly got back to work and flew to Massachusetts with my arm in a sling for Lobsterfest—my second by this point. I was on muscle relaxers and painkillers, and I remember having one drink and catching myself slurring. For a split second I thought, *What the hell am I doing here?* I was burning the candle at both ends and running out of wax. I could wake up on a Saturday, drink a whole pot of coffee, and fall right back to sleep.

When Kara called to talk about our daughter, I was working in my capacity as a case agent back in McAllen and happened to be in an interview room with a suspect.

Our daughter was sick, and Kara was also exhausted. I just kept telling her to take our little girl to the doctor—the money was coming out of my paycheck every month for healthcare anyway, why didn't we use it? But Kara didn't want to bring her to a crowded waiting room with other sick children for hours just for the doctor to say she had a virus. I sighed heavily into the phone.

In my defense, the sigh was because my head was still in the interview room, working the case, but I knew I should probably head home. I was just frustrated with the situation. To Kara, the sigh was me being pissed off. She hung up without another word.

I wrapped up the interview and went right home. When I got there, the fight continued and escalated. We were both sleep-deprived and stressed, and we were both talking, but not really listening. I got madder and madder until I kicked an ottoman, and it went flying across the room, punching a hole in the drywall.

Kara ran to the bathroom and locked herself in. Minutes later, through the door, she told me she had called 911.

"You called 911?"

"Yes. But I hung up."

"It doesn't matter," I said and readied myself. What Kara didn't know was that a 911 call with no response means the cops are coming.

I knew the McAllen police were on their way, so I called my supervisor as I walked outside our home. He was having lunch at the time, and I said as calmly as I could, "I think you better get over here. The cops are coming."

This wasn't my first outburst. A few weeks earlier, someone had run over our beloved dog, a little bichon frise named Tucker. It happened right outside our house, in front of me, and I just saw red. Without thinking and with spit flying from my mouth as I yelled, I walked over to the driver. He was already outside of his truck apologizing. I picked him right up off the ground and slammed him back against his truck.

Tucker survived but was never really the same. The driver was shaken but fine and returned to our house that night to apologize again.

After my outburst I started to really worry about where my head was at. I had always prided myself on my restraint, but I didn't have any that day with the driver. And now I had lost it on Kara, too.

5

THE BASEMENT

Taunton, Massachusetts
November 29, 2006

The Outlaws clubhouse was a cinderblock building nestled in a residential neighborhood and impossible to miss: The Outlaws black flag proudly flew out front, with a driveway full of Harleys.

You'd enter through a heavy, solid door, secured by dead bolts and a metal bar. The floor was that black-and-white diamond tile pattern you sometimes see in old barbershops. There was a well-stocked bar area, and on the walls were framed T-shirts from the other chapters: Georgia, Jacksonville, Milwaukee, Chicago, and a couple international ones like Germany and Belgium. They loved their bumper stickers and graffiti, and the walls were filled with both.

There were signatures from members, and signs that read, "This is not the place to find out you can't handle your alcohol," on the fridge.

Adorning the main doorway frame were "OFFO" and "GFOD" stickers. The OFFO stood for "Outlaws Forever. Forever Outlaws," a pretty standard saying. GFOD was "God Forgives. Outlaws Don't."

Move through that doorframe, past the restroom on the left, and the room opened up to reveal a stage with a stripper pole, a Confederate flag, and lots of mirrors on the walls so the area seemed larger than it was. They also made it impossible to hide anywhere. Fans slowly turned overhead, pushing around stale air that smelled of booze, smoke, testosterone, and leather.

By this time, I had been working about eighteen months undercover on Operation Roadkill and knew that clubhouse well. There was only one door I'd never been through: that *one* door on the right, across from the bathroom. No one had ever asked me to go there until the night of November 29.

—

Over the summer and fall of 2006, I "bought" more than a dozen vehicles from the Outlaws—Harleys, pickup trucks, a black BMW, a gold Nissan Maxima—which were supposedly destined for Mexico but ended up in our FBI garage as evidence. Joe Doggs, Clothesline, and Scott T were the main targets I dealt with, but other members would come in and out of the scene.

To transport the goods, I introduced the Outlaws to "Tony," an FBI undercover agent who posed as another one of my drivers. Like Johnny, who was the first of my truckers Joe Doggs had met, Tony's main undercover role was as a driver, and he definitely knew his way around a semitruck.

On our first deal I could just picture him in his cab cussing me, as I was in my car ahead cussing Joe Doggs. As I would later learn, Doggs was a mess. In addition to never having the collateral to pay me up front, he hadn't even arranged to have the motorcycles all in one place for pickup.

That meant we were driving through residential neighborhoods, negotiating circle drives, narrow streets with low power lines, and cars everywhere. It was conspicuous, and no place for a truck that size.

Our first stop that day was at an apartment complex to pick up a bike that belonged to member Richard Elliott, a.k.a. "Rain." His motorcycle wouldn't crank, so we had to push it a fair distance to the truck and then up the ramp to load. That wasn't a good start. Our second location was Clothesline's house, and I remember waiting there with Joe Doggs until Tony caught up. We could see a good way down the street, before the road dropped off, and watched the top of Tony's truck as it got closer and closer. Then it just stopped. We waited and waited. Finally, Clothesline ran down the street to figure out what was going on and came back to report that Tony had been in a minor wreck, which meant we now had to wait until the cops came and left to finish our deal. Consider it a lesson learned, because the next time we did a deal, I made damn sure Joe Doggs had all of the goods in one place for pickup.

I wasn't the only one now questioning Joe Doggs's ability. Sure, he was still the head of the Taunton chapter, but many of the members were bitching about him. One night, when Clothesline had served his sentence and was back out of jail, he told me about a job they had done a couple weeks before he got arrested. They had gotten a tip about some skinny forty-year-old guy who had $120,000 just sitting in his safe "for the taking." Joe Doggs wasn't Clothesline's first choice for a wingman, but he was the only one available, so he armed himself with a 9mm Beretta, gave Joe Doggs a .38-caliber pistol, and off they went.

"I told him," Clothesline said to me, "if anything goes wrong, blast this motherfucker! Hit him in the knees first. Don't kill him until we get the safe open."[1]

"No problem," Joe Doggs replied. Then there was a problem.

Subduing the scrawny guy (who was caught totally unprepared) wasn't an issue. Clothesline got him on his stomach and had his zip ties in his hand. Then the guy turned over. And suddenly there was a gun pointed right at Clothesline's chest.

Click.

He pulled the trigger.

Click.

He pulled the trigger again, but the gun didn't fire. "Shoot him! Shoot him!" Clothesline shouted as he hammered the man. But Doggs just stood there, immobile. He was having what Clothesline described as a panic attack. As Clothesline tried to get his own gun, the skinny guy escaped and ran out the door screaming, "Call the cops! They're trying to kill me!"

You'd think maybe Clothesline would consider this near-death moment as divine intervention; a version of that scene from *Pulp Fiction* when Samuel L. Jackson looked at the bullet-riddled wall behind them and then turned to John Travolta to proclaim: "God came down from heaven and stopped these motherfuckin' bullets."

Instead, Clothesline sat there shaking his head as he told me this story. "When shit hit the fan," he said, "he wasn't there to back me up."

—

Joe Doggs never stopped talking about transporting drugs. From day one, he looked to me as a possible supplier, especially since I lived close to the Mexican border. And by now, they were starting to trust my criminal bona fides and I had lined their pockets with cash from our vehicle deals.

One of the hardest requirements when building these cases is patience. You can't look too eager or obvious, or they'll quickly smell a rat. I had to very slowly—week by week—expand my legend with small breadcrumbs and let them know, well yes, I *did* used to deal with the cartels to help them distribute drugs throughout the United States. I explained the reason that the cartels dealt with a gringo like me and never cut me out was because *I* was the guy with the contacts at the ports of entry and checkpoints. As soon as the drugs arrived at the border, I could get the trucks across by paying corrupt border agents $10,000 to $15,000 per vehicle. Then I would make sure the shipment was safe in the U.S. and reached the intended dealers. I tried not to work in Mexico because of the risks, I told the guys. Los Zetas were the Gulf cartels' enforcers, and I always worried about kidnappings.

The only reason I stopped transporting drugs was because there had been too much heat in recent years and a couple of my crew were popped by law enforcement. I let them sit with those stories for a few weeks.

After enough time had passed, I casually mentioned that "Manny" had reached out. Manny was my old cartel contact and wanted me back in the game. He told me he had a shipment destined for Canada and needed my protection. But the Canadian buyers no longer had their contacts at the northern border, so I told Manny I wasn't willing to risk my drivers getting caught. Manny had a proposal: What if he could get the Canadians to meet us in the U.S. Could I transport the drugs safely to them?

That was pretty much all I had to say. Joe Doggs was in.

This drug deal would take the investigation to the next level. We would be transporting forty kilograms of cocaine and a thousand pounds of marijuana, with a street value of more than a million dollars. And it would be the real stuff, too. Which meant we had to envision the dozens of different scenarios where things could go wrong.

A couple days before the deal, I met the FBI Boston SWAT team preparing for the operation. I walked into their field office right as a briefing was taking place. Projected on the wall behind me were photos of Joe Doggs, Clothesline, and the other targets, and pictures of where the deal would go down with a bunch of arrows. As I turned from the wall, all I could see was the projector's bright light and a dark room.

"Please don't shoot this guy," I said, grinning, thumbs pointing to my chest.

As the lights went up, a few familiar faces from the SWAT team came into focus. I listened in as they laid out their contingency plans. The team would consist of a couple dozen agents, including hidden snipers, loads of surveillance, and, of course, covert backup. One of the biggest concerns was how to react if the targets tried to rip off the dope. What if Joe Doggs or any of the members got stupid enough to turn on me and try his luck with the "cartel"?

Aside from this backup, we would also have a team of undercover agents helping with the operation. In addition to my driver Tony, there were several others posing alongside Manny as part of the cartel, as well as undercovers pretending to be Canadian buyers.

It was surreal moving between teams, but when in character, I was fully that person—as Scott Payne checking in with my FBI team; as Scott Callaway checking in with my Outlaws targets. One message was the same to both the hunters and the hunted, though: Things needed to go according to plan.

I told Joe Doggs and the others who would provide protection detail for the drug shipment that they needed to be ready to roll by 11 a.m. on Thursday, November 30, 2006.

But the night before, I got a call to come to the clubhouse.

—

Life with Kara had calmed since my outburst. That was thanks to her patience and our faith. When I was home, we would host a Christian "small group" at our house. If you're not familiar with small group, it's essentially a gathering of close-knit Christians who meet once a week to support each other and talk through problems and learn from the Bible's teachings. Danny Price, the number two pastor at Baptist Temple Church in McAllen at the time, would lead our small group. I couldn't go into all the details of my work, but the small group knew I was an undercover agent and all the stresses it entailed. I really credit the group with keeping our marriage together during those rocky weeks.

I wouldn't alter my appearance while undercover (hey, I *was* a biker who liked my tattoos and jeans), but when I came back home, there were always two small changes I made. I'd take off the cheap wedding ring I bought and wore after I got "married" undercover and put my real wedding band back on. It had "Love, Kara" and our wedding date engraved on it. I would also take off the skull on my necklace and put my cross back on. One day Kara noticed that the skull was still hanging around my neck, even though I'd been home for a while. It felt like a scary sign. *Was I just tired, or was it getting harder to see the difference between the two Scotts?*

Years later, she told me that she believed her job was to keep our homelife as calm as possible, and the moment I stepped out of the door, to cover me in prayers. I was so overcome by gratitude for her when she said this, and it really hit home the toll my job had taken on her. But that insight, as I said, came years later. At the time, my vision was tunnel-focused on the case.

When Joe Doggs called me to come to the clubhouse on November 29, there were no red flags. I knew they'd be jittery about the deal and probably wanted to go over the plan again. Besides, it helped me because the U.S. Attorney's Office was always looking for more evidence and encouraged me to get them to talk about the deal inside the clubhouse.

But when I arrived, I did start to wonder what was going on. Joe Doggs wasn't picking up his phone. I knocked on the clubhouse door. A few seconds later, the door opened, but no more than a few inches, just enough to see Joe Doggs looking a little nervous and telling me to come back. They were still conducting business at church, he told me.

I wasn't a patched Outlaw, so I didn't expect to be invited in for church. But I did wonder why he had called me to come at that time if he wasn't ready to see me. Joe Doggs asked me to take Obie (Steven O'Brien Jr., a probationary member) to nearby Lombardi's Bar. Then we waited outside the clubhouse until Joe Doggs called me back. I noted the time for the report I knew I'd later write. It was 8:35 p.m.

Inside the clubhouse I slipped into my usual jovial Tex mode, cracking jokes. A drink was being poured for me when Clothesline said, "Tex. Can I talk to you for a minute?" It was more of a command than a question. Then he walked toward one door I'd never been through.

I followed, holding a plastic cup with my Jack and Coke. We walked down the steps, and I learned that this door led to the clubhouse basement, although calling it a basement was generous since it was about the size of a big broom closet, with a ceiling so low I couldn't stand up straight.

As I slowly descended the steps with Clothesline, Scott Bulgar, a.k.a. Chocolate Scott, moved in behind me. It was dark and cramped and I was getting nervous. *What the fuck was happening?*

"Uh, should I ask what's going on?" I asked Clothesline, my voice tight and high.

"No. Just precautions. That's all," he replied. "There's a lot of shit going on. It's my job to take care of all my brothers. All right?"

Chocolate Scott stayed on the stairs, his arms resting on the low wall just above his head, his pistol in his waistband clearly exposed. He was blocking my way out.

I looked around the tiny basement and saw a rope, and noted Clothesline also had his gun. But there wasn't any plastic on the floor. If I had seen plastic, I'm not sure what I would have done, except maybe try to fight my way out, and likely die in a blaze of glory.

Then Clothesline asked me to write down my full name and my address on a piece of paper. He told me to take off all my clothes because he had to "check me out." I'm not going to lie, by this point, my asshole had started knitting a sweater.

I was so stressed I even forgot what my fake middle name was. Carefully, I wrote "Scott Callaway," and to give myself some time, I asked, "And what else do you need. Name? And what else?" I was just trying to distract them and remember my damn middle name. Clothesline said to Chocolate Scott, "Why don't you ask Keith what he needs for that site?" Keith Michonski, who was upstairs, was another probationary member.

My mind was whirling. I figured, they're putting my data into one of those websites that tracks agents or snitches. There was a popular one at the time called whosarat.com. As they're yelling to each other, my mind is racing. *Scott Callaway? Scott Joseph Callaway. Joseph? Fuck no. Joseph was a name I used before.*

My body was reacting physically to the massive adrenaline dump. I could feel my hamstrings get rubbery and every thump of my heartbeat. My senses went into overdrive and time dilation meant my vision started to look like a dreamy movie trailer. *Click, click, click.* I felt the auditory exclusion, as sound became distorted, and it felt like I was underwater. *Whoosh, whoosh, whoosh.*

Then it hit me: *Andrew.* I remembered I thought it was funny to have the initials "SAC," which in the land of FBI acronyms means special agent in charge. I wrote it down.

"Do you understand what I'm getting at?" Clothesline asked me as Chocolate Scott shifted behind me.

"I mean, we've already done business," I said to Clothesline, trying to steady my voice, which suddenly sounded a pitch higher to me.

I was praying hard, looking for a sign. Clearly, I wasn't listening. Had I been, I would have heard that the Lynyrd Skynyrd song *Gimme Three Steps* was playing in the clubhouse the entire time I was in there! It's a song about a guy in a bad situation desperately trying to get to the door to get out.

I was equipped with my standard video and recording devices, as usual. As I've said previously, I can't go into detail about exactly where they were on my body or what they looked like, but let's just say a strip search definitely risked my cover.

Slowly I took my jacket off, my shirt, then my boots. I dropped my pants and underwear around my ankles. Clothesline continued to talk.

"Cases have been built against people . . ." He trailed off, then added, "Trust me. If someone was accusing me of being a fucking fed, I would smash them in the fucking mouth."

"I'm not happy," I replied, but I was staring right at Clothesline with a look that I hoped was saying, *Tell me we're okay.*

"I know you're not happy," he said. "I wouldn't be either."

I tried to sound casual again. "It's all right . . . You're doing your deal, bro."

"What would you do if someone came to your town and started doing all types of shit with you, wouldn't you be suspect?" Clothesline asked.

"Yeah, if they came to me," I protested. "But I didn't come to nobody. People *came to me.*"

There was a pause. I willed my breathing to slow again.

"Am I good?" I asked.

Clothesline was smiling. "Yeah."

"Well, can you hug me now?" I laughed, maybe a little too enthusiastically. I pulled my pants back up, and I started coming back into my body as a wave of relief washed over me.

Then Clothesline picked up my jacket. We weren't done. *Click. Click. Click. Whoop. Whoop. Whoop.*

"You got anything in your jacket you don't want me to find . . . Like some pictures of my old lady?"

I laughed and he joined me. I muttered, "I don't know. I hope not." Then I inadvertently let out a low groan wearier and more scared than maybe any sound I'd ever made in my life. I sounded like a wounded animal.

Clothesline was kneading my jacket, running his hands up and down the sleeves, the buttons. If he had felt anything and asked, "What is this?" I only had two responses: "I don't know. Naked pictures of your old lady?" If that didn't work, I only had one option left: "The gig's up. I'm an undercover FBI agent. I can walk out of here and we can see each other in court, or all hell's gonna break loose." The problem was, I may have been bluffing, because I wasn't sure if my cover team could hear me at all.

I stood there shirtless as I watched him continue groping my jacket. It felt like forever.

Then he handed it back. And just like that, it was over.

"I gotta do what I gotta do," Clothesline said, looking almost as relieved as I was.

I muttered in response, "No hard feelings. That's cool. That's cool."

Then we climbed out of the basement.

—

My cover team at the beginning of the shift that night consisted of Brockton Police Department Detective Joe Cummings and Massachusetts State Trooper Sergeant Thomas Higginbotham. What I didn't know at the time, but would find out later that night as I handed in my recording equipment, was that something hadn't sat right with them the moment Joe Doggs refused my entry into the clubhouse.

Once I was inside, Higginbotham and Cummings moved close enough to hear me. They heard every word, and when I was taken down to the basement, they radioed the FBI's Boston office, telling them I was wired up and the Outlaws were stripping me. That meant action. The blue lights and sirens were coming.

Higginbotham and Cummings, as local law enforcement, had been in that clubhouse on search warrants before and knew the layout. They quickly decided that ramming the van through the wall beside the door would be an easier way to breach the clubhouse, rather than trying to get through the fortified door. They suited up, vests on, and continued to listen. Listening as my voice got higher. Listening as Clothesline talked.

I can't say enough good things about Cummings and Higginbotham. They had the wherewithal and experience, and after a year and a half on the case, they knew me well. One thing you're always taught as an undercover, and what I now teach new recruits, is to never vapor lock—always keep talking, keep gathering intel, keep listening. They were ready to pull the trigger, but they didn't, and because of their savviness, they saved the case.

Timothy Quinn, who was the FBI case agent, had just started his shift in the Boston office when Cummings and Higginbotham radioed in to say I was in trouble. Quinn, who was born and raised in New Jersey, was not only an excellent case agent, he had also been my best friend at the FBI Academy. We stayed at his parents' place when he took me to New York for the first time to help me find a place to live. I remember him saying to me later that night of the strip search, "When I was coming down that highway, signal one, blue lights and sirens on, man, I felt like I was in there with you." I replied with a grin, "Um, you weren't."

By the time I was finally on my way back to my hotel, with only a few hours left before I had to be up again, I called Kara on the burner phone I'd given her—the one I used to check in at the end of each night, whether it was 4 a.m. or seven in the morning.

She immediately asked me, "Are you okay?"

I told her I was and asked, "Why?"

Then she said that earlier in the evening she was driving with the girls in McAllen and was struck with an overwhelming feeling. She pulled over to the side of the road and started praying for me.

I asked her what time that was. It was the exact time I was being stripped in the basement.

6

THE CRASH

Brockton, Massachusetts
November 30, 2006

"Nobody late. Nobody gets nervous. Nobody fucks around."

When you talk to the cartel, you talk with respect. I had been delivering that message to Joe Doggs and his crew for weeks now. Today was finally the day.

I eased my rental car off Route 44 and into the IHOP parking lot to meet Doggs that Thursday morning with Scott T and Obie along as passengers. I was fueled by adrenaline, caffeine, and about an hour of sleep since my basement strip search.

I had told the guys not to wear any colors for the deal—just dress as plainly as possible so as not to draw attention. Joe Doggs was in the parking lot wearing a baseball cap backward, and his white hoodie with blue flames up the sleeves unzipped to expose a T-shirt that screamed in all caps, "FUCK THAT BITCH." *That's not drawing attention?*

He slipped a pistol that he was lending to me for the deal into my car, and together we went across the street to the Radio Shack to buy six handheld radios so we could communicate without being overheard by law enforcement. By the time we got back to the IHOP parking lot, Scott Bulgar, a.k.a. Chocolate Scott (and sometimes Black Scott); Eddie Bullio, a member of the Outlaws Brockton chapter; and Tony Lima had arrived. Lima was on probation with the Outlaws, and like all probies had been assigned a sponsor; Spanky was his "dad," but did not want to be part of this deal. The only member of the team we were now missing was Clothesline.

We gathered around Chocolate Scott's car as he sat in the driver's seat taking long drags on his cigarette. I leaned in, my voice low, but loud enough for the recording equipment to pick up our conversation as I outlined where the deal would go down. I told them we would be responsible for moving a shipment of cocaine and marijuana from the cartel's truck into the Canadian buyer's truck. But we needed to be patient. "When one truck backs up to the other, that's quick. But the money's in a different location. The money has to be counted before we do anything," I told them. "We're going to the Westgate Mall, all right?"

At that point, Chocolate Scott, who lived just blocks from that mall, interrupted me, banging his hand on the steering wheel. "I could have stayed at fucking home for that, man! I could have slept another hour!" I watched as Joe Doggs started rocking slightly, shifting his weight impatiently from his left foot to his right as he gulped from a water bottle. "You all are the laziest bunch of criminals I've ever met in my life, man," he yelled, a little too loudly. "I swear to God!"[1]

They continued to bitch back and forth, until I got us back on track. "Would you shut the fuck up and listen so we can get on the road?" I pulled out a piece of paper from my vest, which had a rough, hand-drawn map that highlighted the parking lot of the Brockton Holiday Inn and the Westgate Mall. I told Scott T, Joe Doggs, and Obie they would be with me, in the hotel parking lot with our trucks. Bullio, Lima, and Chocolate Scott would be on lookout, positioning themselves at the three entrances into the Westgate Mall. "All I need: Number one, be patient until we get the money counted and everything and then everything's going to be good," I told them. Once I got the signal that the money was all there, we could transfer the drugs and get out of there. We'd get our cut later.

"But don't panic if you see fucking Five-O," I warned. "You just call it in. Because if Five-O's seen, I don't want anybody leaving their spots, because all we're going to do is shut the doors on the trucks and the trucks are going to pull apart from each other. Okay? And we're gonna wait." Scott T would be in charge of the radios, and Joe Doggs and Obie would be inside the trucks, transferring the cocaine and marijuana from one to the other.

There was still no sign of Clothesline, but we couldn't delay any longer. We left the parking lot and arrived at the Westgate Mall just before noon. As we waited there for the trucks to arrive, Joe Doggs started to get antsy. "Hey yo," he said to me, just minutes before Tony rolled up in our truck. "If these Canadian people do anything dumb, dude, we're just going to riddle them motherfuckers with bullets. Right?"

I assured him everything would go according to plan, and I prayed to God that it would.

—

Chocolate Scott was remarkably good at surveillance and did not budge from his lookout post. At one point, our radios crackled to life as he reported: "Crown Vic. Tinted windows. Occupied two times, headed your way." I looked at Scott T and said something like, "What did he just say??" For a split second I was thinking, *Wait, is Chocolate Scott a cop? Is this blue on blue?* It wouldn't be the first time one law enforcement agency hadn't been talking to another and there were two undercovers on the inside. I knew of several cases in New York where that had happened.

When the trucks came, Joe Doggs and Obie went to work, moving the goods quickly from the "cartel" truck to the "Canadians," after I gave them the go-ahead that the money was all there. Before we wrapped that night, I counted out $15,000 for Joe Doggs to dispense to the team. It may not seem like much for such a big deal, but they were okay with it for now—with hopes of bigger deals to follow.

At that point, we could have wrapped the case against Joe Doggs, Obie, Chocolate Scott, Tony, and Eddie for drug conspiracy. It would have been a good federal indictment. But my cover was still secure, and while we had evidence on other members, too, we wanted to make sure we had an airtight case. The case team and the U.S. Attorney's Office decided Operation Roadkill should keep going.

—

By Friday afternoon, less than forty-eight hours since I was strip-searched in the clubhouse basement, I hopped on a plane back home to McAllen. But due to a strong headwind, I landed late at Houston Airport and missed my connecting flight, which meant I might be late getting to the FBI's Rio Grande Valley Christmas party, where I had an important role to play. "How's it looking?" I asked the first frazzled agent I could talk to as an angry mob of passengers crowded into Small Terminal B. She sighed deeply. "Listen, I'm not going to come up here and cuss. Everybody's mad. But if there's anything you can do, I'd greatly appreciate it," I said to her. "I missed my connecting flight, and if I don't make this next flight, there's going to be a bunch of kids in the Rio Grande Valley that aren't going to get to meet Santa Claus tonight."

She looked around and then said, "No matter what I say, stay right here."

I did as she told me to, and stayed put as she called out the names on the standby list and then announced that the flight was full, and the doors were closing. I waited until the frustrated travelers had snaked their way to the next gate with a flight. Then she came over and said, "Come with me," and the door opened again. I thanked her profusely and boarded.

As soon as I arrived home, Scott Payne was back. I changed my shirt, took the skull off the chain around my neck and replaced it with a cross, switched my wedding rings, brushed my teeth, loaded up Kara, her mother, and our girls, and off we went to the FBI party, where I played Santa Claus for a room full of children.

Ho . . . F'n . . . Ho . . .

By Sunday morning I was on a plane again, flying off for another sleep-deprived couple of weeks instructing at the FBI's Undercover School.

—

Over the course of Operation Roadkill, my relationship with Scott T deepened. It was about as close a friendship as was possible under the circumstances. Don't get me wrong, it's not like I was going to the dark side, but I loved that guy.

I remember one afternoon, just chilling at his place having a beer and bouncing his youngest daughter on my lap, who was the exact age of my youngest girl. They were doing all the same types of movements, using the same verbiage. It was scary how much Scott T and I were alike and all the things we had in common. Just as these thoughts were going through my head, I looked over to his fridge, which was covered with stickers and spotted one that said "WWSD?" *What Would Satan Do?* It snapped me back to reality. Oh right, we *were* different.

I was having similar problems, though, with Clothesline. I was letting feelings that shouldn't come into a case consume me. I took that basement strip search personally and I was pissed that not only had he betrayed *me*, but then he'd had the nerve to not show up for the deal the next day. I had left Massachusetts without talking to him. It would be another three months until we were again face-to-face.

I finally did see him on that cold February evening as he walked into one of the Outlaws' hangouts, Tony's Cantina, and came over to me as I was sitting with some of the other Outlaws members, I could feel myself getting tense again. I knew I'd have to talk with him about all that had happened, but I had no idea where it would go.

"Hey, Tex," he said. "You got a minute?"

"I'm not sure I do, Clothesline," I replied, the irritation still in my voice. "The last time you asked me that I ended up in a basement naked." He assured me this was different, so I followed him to the back.

Clothesline looked beaten down, a little sad, and he started to slowly explain what had led to our basement encounter; how word had come down from Outlaws National president Jack Rosga, a.k.a. "Milwaukee Jack," to check me out. He said he really didn't want to do it and felt like shit. And he claimed that he pushed back, saying that he and other members had already done a bunch of deals with me and weren't in "bracelets." But an order was an order, and he was the chapter's enforcer. That night after I left the clubhouse, he was so messed up about what had happened, he got trashed out of his mind, and he slept through the entire deal the next day.

I was listening, of course, but I was still upset, and my face showed it. Clothesline continued to look somber. "Look, man, I know I was born to be an outlaw. And I know I'm either going to die young or I'm going to die in prison." He paused. "Even though these guys are my brothers, I really don't have a lot of friends. Friends that I would take a bullet for and I know would take a bullet for me." My expression softened, and I started thinking, *Don't you say it. Don't . . . you . . . fucking . . . say it.*

Then he said it.

"And you're one of those guys."

When I called Kara that night to check in, she asked how my day went. "I'm a dick. I'm a dick. I'm such a dick," I said in despair. "This guy loves me."

—

The FBI has a unit known as "Safeguard," which was developed to preserve "the safety, security, and psychological well-being" of undercover agents, but was later expanded to include other personnel working on psychologically taxing cases.[2] As an active undercover, you are required to be assessed periodically. If things get crazy, you can be ordered to be assessed at any time (such as the time when Kara called 911 or when I was stripped in the basement).

I would always tell them I was doing fine and managing the stress well. No one was pushing me to do more—I was taking on all the work because I liked it. It was exhausting, sure, but I was holding it together and not feeling any pressure. At the time, I had no real idea how I was breaking down.

I was scheduled for an assessment right before my next meeting with the Outlaws, this time at a motorcycle rally in Daytona, Florida, in March 2007. I landed early in Orlando to meet the Safeguard team at their hotel.

One of the psychological tests we had to complete as part of an assessment was a series of fill-in-the-blank questions. I answered them as I usually would. But then I got to one that stated: *The last time I relaxed I* ________, and my mind went blank. I couldn't think of a single thing I was doing to relax. Sure, I still worked out, but it wasn't like I was listening to Yanni and doing yoga. For just a moment, I thought, *Well, that's pretty messed up.* I had my minor in psychology (two more classes and I could have had a double major), and I recognized that sure wasn't a good sign. But I quickly blew it off.

Instead, I wrote about a day trip I took to South Padre Island about an hour east of McAllen with Kara and the girls. But those trips usually weren't relaxing. There was the stressful drive along Highway 83, which runs parallel to the Mexican border. Then I'd watch my daughters with eagle eyes while at the beach, unable to lay back even for a second. The day would usually end with dinner and the family sound asleep as I drove us home. Exhausting. But that was my answer, and off I went.

—

Like the Sturgis Bike Rally, Daytona's annual Bike Week in March has been going on for decades, drawing hundreds of thousands of motorcycle enthusiasts. We were getting toward the end of our Boston case, but Daytona was going to be a great chance to gather even more intelligence, and meet Outlaws from all over the U.S. It was considered a "mandatory ride," which meant all Outlaws had to show up, and I had been invited.

I arrived before the others from Massachusetts rolled into town, so I decided to ride by the Daytona Outlaws clubhouse on my own, just to take a look. The palm tree–lined Beach Street was packed, motorcycles slowly crawling along or parked on the side. Almost directly in front of the clubhouse I spotted a familiar figure—tall, bald, bushy sideburns, and that distinct cross-and-hammer tattoo on his neck. *Hillbilly.*

Hillbilly was once the president of the Jacksonville chapter, and had recently been promoted to southeast regional president. He was also the first skinhead to join the Outlaws and had actively recruited members from the white supremacist movement. (Although curiously he was one of the main ones to vouch for Chocolate Scott, who you may have guessed got his nickname due to his darker skin, although he denied he had any African American heritage.)

I'd gotten to know Hillbilly in Massachusetts when he came to visit. On one scouting mission the previous fall, I drove around with my arm in a sling from my shoulder surgery, Joe Doggs in the passenger's seat and Hillbilly in the back. We were doing some reconnaissance for the next stolen vehicle pickup and talking in shitty code. Hillbilly stopped us. "Hey, you guys, stop talking about this shit. I don't want to be part of y'all's conspiracy!" I thought this was one of the funniest things and started laughing. Hillbilly knew his law, and he was right, even being in the car and privy to our conversations could make him party to a federal conspiracy.

In Florida, I made eye contact and revved my bike. "Tex? Tex!" he shouted, and I nodded. He pointed to a spot right in front of the clubhouse door where I should park, and I did a U-turn and backed in. As I was parking, Hillbilly joked, "Hey don't be bringing any of that stolen shit around here." I replied, "This isn't stolen, I just borrowed it off a guy down the street." We hugged and he led me inside. Hillbilly walked me right to the bar and told the server to give me whatever I wanted.

It didn't matter that I'd been with the Taunton Outlaws now for nearly two years, this was a whole new scene, and I was being scrutinized and vetted in real time from all corners. As Hillbilly walked me around, I'd introduce myself, "I'm Tex. Taunton, Massachusetts, hang-around. And . . . I'm kind of a Brockton hang-around. I guess . . . I'm kind of a Jacksonville hang-around." Hillbilly interrupted me: "He's the . . . I-get-around hang-around."

Hillbilly was giving me a VIP tour, which included going to the outside tented area, behind the clubhouse. As far as I knew, only fully patched members were allowed there. I stood, sipping my drink as Hillbilly chatted with three other Outlaws, one of whom was really upset about an incident with the Hells Angels and was talking about retaliation. "Look, man, be patient. They expect you to retaliate now. You'll get yours," Hillbilly said, then added, "Look how long I had to wait to get mine up north."

Bear? I couldn't believe what I was hearing. Was Hillbilly just confessing to the 2006 murder of Hells Angels leader Roger Mariani? We knew the shooters were Outlaws from Florida, and I suspected they had gone out with Scott T and Clothesline before the hit, but the case remained unsolved. I took a long gulp of my drink.

That night, I briefed the Boston and Jacksonville FBI teams in a hotel room, explaining all that had happened that day. One of the FBI agents from Florida couldn't believe Hillbilly's candor, saying they had a patched source and Hillbilly did not talk like that around him. He asked the Boston team where they were in their investigation—and they told him we were pretty much ready to wrap the case. Would they consider, he asked, delaying the arrests, and I come down to Florida and attempt to patch under Hillbilly? My answer was always the same—hell yes! I had no idea what was coming.

The next morning, I sat in my hotel room, my sinuses screaming, my stomach sloshing with whiskey and scrambled eggs, and I felt like a zombie. I started with a couple cups of the strongest coffee I could brew, hit my inhaler, took a couple prescription decongestants and an ephedrine supplement. Time to work out: burpees, mountain climbers, push-ups, crunches, and body squats.

After a couple rounds, I came up for air and I couldn't find it. It felt like all the oxygen had been sucked out of the room and my lungs had collapsed. I struggled to breathe. I started to panic as I gulped furiously. Sweat poured down my face and body as I was overcome by a feverish chill.

Knock knock.

I somehow managed to walk to the door, panting, and opened it up to see Tony standing there. Tony had come to Florida with me to be on standby, in case I needed some assistance on the case. I could tell by the look on his face that I did not look well, and he asked if I was okay.

We went out to the balcony, taking in the ocean air, and I tried to calm myself as Tony tried to figure out what was going on. He was a seasoned undercover with a lot of experience.

"Sometimes you feel anxious about the case ending."

"Sometimes you feel anxiety about betraying the friendships you've created."

"Sometimes you feel you're worried they'll find out who you are."

I know he was trying to help and normalize my stress, but the more he talked the more anxious I got about every scenario he suggested. "Could it be any of that?" I laughed. "Well, it is now!"

After Tony left, I took a nap. Should I have gone home or taken some days off? Maybe. But I didn't. I went back to work.

—

I rode out for the night along East International Speedway Boulevard in Daytona with several Outlaws, including Spanky, and a newly patched Taunton member we called "Schultz" (for his resemblance to Sgt. Schultz from *Hogan's Heroes*).

As our destination, Sharky's Lounge, came into view, I was thankful because I could use a good meal. But as we parked under the neon sign with a shark curled around it and I saw the ads for dancers and cheap booze, I realized, ah, it wasn't a restaurant, it was a strip club. So instead, once inside, we started drinking, and it wasn't long before a dancer offered me a dance. I knew I was being watched by all the Outlaws I didn't know yet, so I happily bought one. Extra $10 for the VIP section? Why not?

She led me past a massive bouncer, to a darkened room in the back, with partitioned areas so small that both my arms were hitting the thin-paneled siding. I was barely in my seat before the dancer dropped to her knees, pulled out a condom, and tried to unzip my pants. Then I realized . . . *Oh, this isn't just a strip club. It's a brothel!* The flimsy "wall" beside me started to thump, hitting my shoulder, *pow, pow, pow,* as one of the Outlaws on the other side began to moan. I started talking quickly and ended up paying the dancer more to *not* have sex with me.

I went back out to the bar, not revealing what I'd done and hoping the dancer wouldn't either. The party was in full swing, with Schultz proudly earning his "brown wings." Earning your wings meant performing some sort of sex act with a witness. There were various colors, with various meanings. Brown meant performing analingus with a woman. Yes, this was my life.

I left Daytona with Tony, exhausted, driving back to Orlando to catch my flight home. With all the adrenaline starting to fade, the trip to the airport felt like a blur, as if it was a scene in a movie I once saw. I passed out right at wheels up and slept straight through until the wheels hit the ground in Houston. Same on the connecting flight to McAllen—asleep from wheels up to wheels down. Then I walked in the door at home and went to bed for twelve hours straight, woke briefly, ate, and then back to sleep. Around 9 p.m., Kara woke me up, asking if I was going to eat dinner. Dinner? I couldn't believe I had slept that long. I guessed that I wouldn't be able to fall back to sleep anytime soon . . . but . . .

For a whole week, I averaged over sixteen hours of sleep a day. I wasn't sick and I wasn't depressed. I knew what those both felt like. On Friday morning, a buddy of mine, who was one of the best undercovers I'd ever known, called about another possible biker case. He asked, "How you doin', Country?" I answered honestly, "Not too good." By the end of our hour-long call, he had me convincing myself that I needed to contact Safeguard. I called one of the psychologists that evening and said, "I don't know what's going on, but I think I'm crashing."

Two weeks later, a Safeguard psychologist and counselor flew out to McAllen to do an on-site assessment. I had been nervous about their visit and was reading all the recommended books about stress, thinking about how to answer whatever they threw at me. I remember arriving at their hotel as they were still having breakfast, and getting coffee. I sat before them, my arms locked straight and gripping the table as I did some shallow chest-breathing, the perfect picture of someone who is definitely not relaxed.

The counselor was a buddy of mine, who I'd known through the undercover program. He and psychologist Meredith Krause put me through the assessment. I had all the answers prepared in my head. I was ready to get back to work.

Then my friend said he wanted to do something different. "Scott, let's switch places. Pretend you're me and I'm you. What would you tell me?"

I hadn't prepared for that question. I lowered my head. I took a deep breath.

"I would tell you that you need to take a break and should have taken one a long time ago."

—

3/21/07

I woke up feeling nervous and weird. I had my shake and once my stomach was full, I had a hard time breathing. (Deep breaths.) After medication, I did breathing exercises for 15 minutes and read an anxiety book, which sometimes causes anxiety!! And the Bible, which calmed me down. Feelings—Anxious, afraid, wondering why Ativan isn't kicking this; wondering how long it's going to take to get back to a normal regimen; realizing when I feel short of breath, I don't like it dark, and I'm afraid to be left by myself.

Once I got out, I felt better, although weak. It's 2:30 p.m. and I still haven't eaten lunch. We'll see how it goes.

I'm not sure if my breathing is allergies. I'm off the chart in this area, but I'm afraid to take any medicine because it "jacks" me up. In talking out my problems, I realize that I've been pushing my body too hard for too long. The UC is coming to an end and, maybe, I'm worried about trial and taking down some of the guys I'm close with.

I travel way too much. When I travel, I don't sleep as good + I drink more than I do at home. There have been additional stress factors: My mom's health + surgeries. My wife's stress level when I'm gone. My dad's behavior. Me being stuffed in a basement. I never really decompressed.

Then there's stress at the office when I'm here. (Reactive squad, principal relief, SWAT, training, ADMIN! ADMIN!! ADMIN!!!) I would also like us to get our transfer.

I can handle most of it. I'm going to change several things to relieve some of the pressure + enjoy life. I just can't take it when I feel like I can't breathe, which is fresh in my memory from my panic / hyperventilating episode, two Thursdays ago. I pray for guidance and wisdom to mentally beat this!

—

The Safeguard team diagnosed me as over-assigned. I needed a time-out for a minimum of six months, which is known as a DNR, or "Do Not Recommend."

Reading back now in the diary I wrote in the first month of my DNR, I see that I was scared and focused a lot on my physical health, on just being able to breathe again and not panicking. But I was also gaining perspective, realizing I just had pushed my mind and body too hard without a break. And I was finally starting to see what it was doing to those around me. One of my diary entries read, "Feel like I owe an apology."

I was scared to death and more vulnerable than I'd ever felt before. I was beat down. I wondered how I could ever get back to being as tough as I used to be, while remaining humble to God. And believe me, I was humbled! Then one day while praying, it hit me in the face like a brick. I would have never been who I was, or able to do the things I did *without* God. He blessed me with all of the things that made me who I was.

Operation Roadkill of course continued during this time as the Boston case team was preparing to wrap the investigation. My involvement was limited to phone calls with our targets, no more face-to-face meetings, as the Safeguard team suggested that I discontinue all travel, with the exception of participating in our FBI undercover courses. That's how I found myself on July 30, 2007, in a sweltering city in the southwest.

The city's golden towers rose up from the pavement, shimmering in the unrelenting heat. It was my first time in this city, but I could have been anywhere. My mind that night was thousands of miles away in Massachusetts.

A lot had happened on the case since Daytona. Scotty T called me often during those months, wondering when the hell I would get back to Taunton. It was hard to hear, of course, but I knew I needed to keep working the case the best I could by phone, delay until all the ducks were in a row for the eventual takedown. I made up a story about getting divorced and not being able to live with myself until I had my ex and the kids safely relocated and settled in El Paso, Texas, where her family was.

While I was gone, Scott T finalized plans on the Righteous Few Motorcycle Club (RFMC), which had been approved by Milwaukee Jack to be the number one support club to the Outlaws in the Boston area. I had helped Scott T create the colors, met his VP, and he asked me to serve as the club's "sergeant at arms." I assured Scott T that I would be back soon to fulfill my position and move there once the wife and kids were okay in El Paso.

During these last few months, Joe Doggs, as usual, had problems. He called me pleading to find him four kilograms of cocaine after a drug deal went bad, as he needed to supply those who had already paid him. He was offering me $14,000 per kilogram and promised he had the "cash on hand."

Then there was Timothy J. Silvia, a.k.a. Big T.

Big T was the former president of the Brockton Outlaws chapter and had come on the scene right near the end of the case, once he was released from prison on a drug conviction. Scott T had introduced me to him, before my DNR. Big T wanted back in the game.

Big T had led a troubled life—grade six education and in and out of jail since he was a teenager. He was in more serious fights and motor vehicle accidents than he could even remember.[3] He had never married, never claimed to be in love, and trusted me as soon as we met. Big T was all about making money and had heard about my reputation of unloading motorcycles, trucks, cars, and drugs south of the border.

While I was in McAllen, he called me often, saying he had purchased a Hummer H-2 that he wanted to report stolen, after the right amount of time had passed, but he had a seven series Beemer and a Ford F-350 pickup truck ready right now for transport. On one call, he asked if I knew what he did for work, confirming that he was in the "magic powder business." He said if I could get him a price of eighteen a piece ($18,000 for a kilo of cocaine), he had enough to buy eight or ten of them (which would mean about $180,000, but the drugs could then be sold on the street for close to half a million). I immediately relayed to the Boston case team that Big T was not only ready to sell me some insurance scam vehicles, but also he was looking to do a drug deal.

On their approval, and from my garage in McAllen, I coordinated a meeting between Big T and "my" truck drivers to unload the vehicles. Tony drove up to Massachusetts along with his passenger, the undercover coordinator of the Boston Division who I'll call "Pete." Pete had accompanied Tony on a few of our previous deals, riding shotgun.

Tony called me to tell me everything was good to go, and to find out how much to pay Big T. Tony then handed the phone to Big T, who had planned on having the BMW reported stolen on Friday. I asked him if he could wait another day, and just until Saturday, because it would for sure be in Mexico by then. When Big T handed the phone back to Tony, I confirmed the $21,000 payout for the vehicles and hung up.

Once I was off the phone, but before Big T left, he took Tony and Pete aside, asking them about the eight to ten kilos. We had it—that would be the final nail in Operation Roadkill's coffin.

Pete met Big T again on June 15, to finalize the drug deal, which they set for July 30, the afternoon I was trying to concentrate on the undercover school. I had meticulously drawn diagrams for all the locations and faxed (yes, faxed, this was 2007) them to SWAT teams throughout the northeast region in preparation for the arrests and search warrants. I wished I was there on the ground with them.

Ironically, I was teaching a block of instruction called "Undercover Stressors" at the time. During my DNR, some longtime undercover mentors who I really respected checked on me to see how I was doing. They told me to take care of myself and my family, and then put pen to paper everything I had learned over the last three years, as they felt what I faced on this case would be a good lesson to others. But the students sitting before me had no idea what I was going through at that very moment—how more than two years of work undercover would come down to these next few hours and all the complicated feelings I had about that.

Then the day got even more surreal: Just as I was in the middle of my class, the door opened and a man walked right up and sat to my right, looking at me. "Speaking of undercover stressors . . . Class, say hello to Mr. Joe Pistone, a.k.a. Donnie Brasco." It was my first time teaching this class, and one of the godfathers of undercover is sitting three feet from me?

At the end of the session, he patted my cheek and kissed me on both sides, mob-style. Then he whispered in my ear, "I'm glad you're okay, kid."

—

In the early morning hours, after the students had gone to bed, I made my way back to my hotel room. The city looked about as weary as I felt. As soon as I opened the door, I could hear my undercover Nextel chirping. I had left the phone in the room to charge, never expecting it to ring again.

It was Scott T.

"Tex, you there?" he said in a gravelly voice. "Hey man, I wanted to let you know I just got contacted. Big T got arrested, your truckers, too. I don't know what's going on, but wanted to let you know," he told me.

I took a breath, and feigned ignorance, saying sometimes my guys did deals on their own. Scott T said he was going to have a shower and try to find out what was going on and call me back. And he cautioned me to stay safe.

"I love you, brother," he said before hanging up.

"I love you, too," I replied.

These were the last words I ever spoke to Scott Callaway's friend. Forty minutes later the SWAT team hit his house.

Operation Roadkill ended with the takedown of fifteen members, in different locations, and all fifteen ended up pleading guilty. Big T and his partner, Todd Donofrio, came to the Holiday Inn parking lot for the deal, and left in handcuffs. They were charged with "conspiracy to possess with intent to distribute cocaine" and "criminal forfeiture allegation." Big T got the stiffest sentence of anyone on Operation Roadkill—twenty-one and a half years. His accomplice, Todd, got a sentence of ten years.

The other thirteen arrested included Scott T, Joe Doggs, Clothesline, Chocolate Scott, Eddie, Obie, Tony Lima, and John Agresta, whose dad owned Tony's Cantina, along with Outlaws John Pombriant, a.k.a. Bones; Jose Espada, a.k.a. Roe; Mark Direnzo, a.k.a. Chooch; and Catherine Larkin, who was a friend of one of the Outlaws. Larkin and Chooch were charged with insurance fraud and got probation, while the rest got varying sentences for convictions of distributing cocaine and possession of a firearm.

Joe Doggs and Clothesline were locked up for twelve and a half years each. Scott T got a sentence of seven years. The cases were pretty much open and shut, no fuss, and I didn't have to testify. I never saw any of the Outlaws again.

7

MARLBORO MAN

Union County, Tennessee
April 30, 2009

The growling redbone hound between my legs was named Bonsey. He had wild eyes, which were fixated on my crotch. The man standing above him, who had a 20-gauge shotgun, with a pistol grip and both hammers cocked on the table within arm's reach, was named Mike Collins. I was cursing myself because I'd neglected one of my own rules: never underestimate a target.

Mike was one reckless, toothless, backwoods country man, but he was savvy and had me jammed into a corner on the couch in his trailer in the Appalachian Mountains of Tennessee.

"If I find out you the law, you're a dead man! You hear me?" he said as he shoved an open bag of cocaine in my face. "If you're not a cop, do it."

And Mike knew cops. He was related to several law enforcement officers. The redbone kept snarling. Mike kept his eyes locked on me.

I tried to talk my way out of it, reminding him that he knew I didn't do coke anymore. I told him I used to be a powerlifter and a speed freak, and since I had panic attacks and heart problems, I just couldn't touch the stuff. (Of course, I didn't really have heart problems, but the rest of it wasn't that far from the truth. Not that I was a "speed freak," but before I had my crash on the Outlaws case, I used to take supplements with ephedrine to help with my workouts, so I knew that jittery feeling.)

There didn't seem to be anything that I could say to Mike that would defuse the situation. He had an answer for everything. He replied that his girlfriend, Sherry, who was with us in his trailer, was on the region's volunteer rescue squad so she was basically a medical expert, and she had given that *same* cocaine to someone on the squad with heart problems that *very* morning. He was fine. What's my problem? I looked over at Sherry, who was also a user and missing several teeth and thought, *Yeah . . . she's the last person I would trust.*

I didn't budge, but I knew this was bad. It was what we'd call in the undercover world "a deteriorating situation." Bonesy growled even louder. "Just taste it then," Mike said as he pushed the bag brimming with white powder in my face.

—

At the end of Operation Roadkill, Kara and I got the transfer we had been hoping for, to Knoxville, Tennessee. I had loved living and working in McAllen, Texas, but the heat was relentless, and I wanted to move back closer to where I grew up in the Southeast.

By all accounts, Operation Roadkill was a great success. Of course, one percenter outlaw motorcycle gangs (OMGs) still exist today throughout the U.S. and beyond. They remain active in various criminal activities. There's even a generational aspect to it, with the torch passed on from fathers to sons. In 2019, more than a decade after our case wrapped, the *Fall River Herald News*[1] reported on a criminal hearing in Fall River, Massachusetts, describing it like a scene from the television series *Sons of Anarchy*. "With a heightened police presence and members of two rival gangs watching on, Joseph 'JoJo' Noe of the Outlaws Motorcycle Club was found not guilty on all counts of murder and assault and battery with a dangerous weapon in the September 2019 biker brawl that left a rival club member dead outside," the *Herald* article stated. The photo accompanying the story showed a man with his tattooed arms raised in victory, a reddish-blond beard, and a baseball cap worn backward. On his neck he had a tattoo of crossed hammers. The resemblance to his dad, Joe Doggs, was unmistakable. I thought back to the times I had played with Joe Doggs's son, "JoJo," near the Outlaws clubhouse. Makes you really think about how hard it is for some kids to escape their upbringing—so many people are just products of their environment.

But with every case, including ours, key members were taken off the grid for years, and lives were saved before the Outlaws chapters in the Taunton area could build themselves back up again. For our work, we received the public service award from the United States District Attorney of Massachusetts and the Robert Faulkner Memorial Award from the International Outlaw Motorcycle Investigators Association. I was proud of our work, but I knew I had to make some serious changes in *how* I worked to avoid burning out again and save my marriage.

By the time I arrived in Knoxville, I'd done a lot of self-reflection and some counseling and got to understand what led to my crash. Quite simply, I applied the "warrior mentality" to everything. To me, a warrior mentality is a state of mind where you don't let anything stop you. There's nothing that can beat you. That type of drive and positive attitude is actually imperative in my line of work.

The problem is, to be an effective warrior, you also have to take care of yourself. You have to decompress. You *have* to take days off and do things to relax, or you'll just break. And the fault for not doing that for nearly three years was all mine. No one was pressuring me, no one was over-assigning me. I just rarely said no; I sought out every chance I could get, until it caught up with me.

I remember sitting down with a Christian counselor when I was still living in McAllen, and laying out all I'd done in the last few years as an undercover, as a case agent, and as an instructor, and she said, "Oh my goodness, Scott, the average person would have crashed a year and a half ago."

"Thanks," I replied.

She paused, looked at me, and said, "Thanks? That wasn't a compliment."

I still wasn't getting it. "But that means I'm better than average?"

"Good Lord," she replied. "I've got my work cut out for me."

It wasn't an easy road to become an active undercover agent again. I had to prove to Safeguard that I was ready to take on that particular type of stress, that I had set up some trip wires for myself and had a network of support from friends, mentors, and my church, who could help pull me back, or slow me down if I needed it. Until I got smart enough to do it on my own, they would be the ones to tell me, "Scott, you need to say no." Or, "Go home. You can work on it Monday."

Even though I had personally called Safeguard at the end of the Outlaws case to get their help, there were times I clashed with some members of the unit. Essentially, speculation and miscommunication played a large part in the strife.

In the end, if I wanted to be an active undercover again, they insisted that Kara had to get "safeguarded" along with me, which meant she had to meet FBI psychologists and counselors at a location I can't disclose. Kara was so nervous and didn't have any experience with psychological assessments—she wasn't desensitized to my world.

I told her to be completely honest with her feelings. She didn't work for the FBI and had no obligation to them, and I would respect whatever she said. I remember telling her the night before in our hotel room, "If you think I shouldn't be doing undercover, tell them. If you think I should, tell them. If you think they suck, tell them. They can't do anything to you."

But no matter what I said, Kara didn't sleep at all that night. She didn't even have to go, but she did, to support me.

And that's how a couple years after the Outlaws case wrapped, I was back working undercover as Scott Callaway in Tennessee, meeting the likes of Mike Collins and his redbone.

—

Union County is 224 square miles of rolling hills and beautiful lakes in rural Tennessee, about a forty-five-minute drive north of Knoxville, where nearly 100 percent of the population is white, and one-quarter of young people live under the poverty line.[2] But there are also some of the most expensive waterside properties in the state, and Norris Reservoir is one of the prettiest lakes you'll ever see.

By 2009 it was also at the crossroads of our country's opioid epidemic. The drug scene had dramatically changed since I first worked the vice and narcotics squad back in South Carolina. Prescription painkillers like OxyContin, Percocet, and Hydrocodone had hit the streets with a vengeance. Known as "hillbilly heroin," the easily accessible drugs could be crushed and snorted, or shot up for a quick, long-lasting, and incredibly addictive high. Being "pill sick" is what addicts go through when they withdraw, and it looks about as close as you can come to death.

In 2008, 14,800 Americans died of prescription painkiller overdoses, and by the following year that number had jumped to 37,485, marking the first year that more citizens died from drugs than car accidents.[3] By 2021, that number was over 100,000.[4]

I hadn't been stationed in Knoxville for long when an investigation was opened into public reports about dirty deputies and local cops dealing drugs in the area. But source reporting usually went something like this:

I know for a fact so-n-so's dirty and they're selling dope.

Okay, how do you know?

Because Roger's sister's daughter's boyfriend says...

There was a lot of reporting, which may be enough to open a case, but it wasn't enough to convict someone.

The case team in Knoxville had been working hard at developing sources before I arrived, and one afternoon in 2009, I accompanied FBI Agent K. T. Harper and Tennessee Bureau of Investigation Agent Mark Irwin to meet one. I'll call the source "Garth." Now, Garth had a steady supply of prescribed Oxy80s and Roxy30s, drank beer, was about five-foot-four, hardly ever wore a shirt in the summer, and had a voice way deeper than mine (and I've got a deep voice). Garth was also easy to be around, and he really took to me, and I took to him and his family.

After that meeting, I debated with the case team about going undercover because Garth said he wanted to work with me. I had to weigh my options, though. I'd never been deep undercover so close to home, which had its risks. On the other hand, I'd only been in Tennessee for about six months, so I hadn't had much exposure.

I asked Garth if our targets stayed close to home, and he reassured me that they never traveled out of the hills of Union County to go into the city. After talking it over at home and with the team, I agreed to jump in. We called the case "Poetic Justice," as a little nod to the dirty cops we were targeting.

For my legend, I stuck with the name Scott Callaway because it hadn't been burned for the Outlaws case. The Outlaws all knew me as "Tex," or Scott, but with the exception of that one time during the basement strip search, when Clothesline got me to write out my full name, no one had bothered with it.

I was determined this time, though, not to be a biker. I didn't care if I was a truck driver or a landscaper, just not a biker. It was an effort to not get pigeonholed into one role—I just wanted to expand my undercover portfolio after the Outlaws case. I settled on being a wholesale furniture distributor, which gave me the ability to travel and explain my absences when I was actually home, less than an hour south, with my family. But I also needed something to give me the reputation of being a criminal. I had to start small, so as not to raise suspicions or worry that I was competing with other drug dealers in the area. I decided that stolen goods would be my trade.

Garth had introduced me to Mike Collins, who was one of our targets with relatives in law enforcement. When I first met Mike, he asked me to go for a walk with him, and down we went beside this beautiful creek. Mike was decked out in a Harley-Davidson shirt and hat, and he had a biker wallet and boots, and sure enough one of the first questions he asked was, "Do you ride?"

I replied, "Yep!"

Oh well, I thought to myself, *I guess I'm gonna be a biker again after all.*

Mike was actually a pretty funny guy to be around—until he wasn't—and then he was as mean and unpredictable as his redbone hound. He lived in a one-bedroom trailer on the side of a rural road with Bonesy and Sherry. I remember one day walking in and seeing an itty-bitty TV perched on top of the massive one that ran along one wall of their living room. It was a huge TV, probably sixty inches and heavy as hell, not like the lightweight big televisions we have today that you can pick up with two fingers. There was a big hole right in the middle of it.

"What the hell happened, Mike?" I asked.

"I shot it," he said, as if it made all the sense in the world. He explained that he had been in a fight with Sherry, and I guess instead of shooting her, he shot the television.

I eased into my role as a guy who could sell or trade stolen goods by one day dropping off a master case of cigarettes at Mike's place—which is sixty cartons. I told Mike the stolen cigarettes were left over from my latest deal, and if he could help me sell them that would be great. I charged him $1,200 for the sixty cartons. He could sell them for whatever he wanted and keep the profits (that meant he paid me $20 a carton, which at the time cost about $50). Then I left briefly to go buy us a case of beer.

While I was driving, maybe a mile or two up the road, my cellphone rang. It was Mike. He wanted to see if I could get some more cases, so naturally I said no problem. "What you want? Bud Light, Miller Lite?" I asked, thinking that of course he was talking about the beer I was picking up. "No, no," he says, "cigarettes." "They're already gone??!" I replied, incredulous. I had been out of there no more than five minutes.

I soon discovered there wasn't a problem in Union County getting dope or pills. They were everywhere. But stolen cigarettes that you could get for a cheap price were an untapped market, and no one wanted to pay full price for their smokes. I had picked the perfect niche to ingratiate myself, and as my reputation grew, I acquired a nickname: the Marlboro Man.

After a few months undercover, I could pull up to the back of Judy's Bar and sling cartons off my truck for about $20 to $25 each, bartering and gathering important intel for the case. The dealing got so popular, there would sometimes be a lineup in the parking lot, and I'd just hope the local cops—the clean ones—didn't stop by.

One of the hardest parts for me was finding a way to keep track of all the illegal deals, so I developed a code to punch into my flip phone that I could later record into my reports of who was buying what, and for how much.

Sometimes the targets wouldn't pay me in cash, but trade in opioids and other illegal narcotics. I would be offered two Oxy80s for a carton instead of $20. Of course, those pills would be worth way more than $20, roughly about $160 street value at the time. But that's just how easy it was to get pills in Union County back then.

Slowly, we were building the case, and I was getting closer to the targets and their law enforcement pals.

By that April day in 2009, I was pretty comfortable with Mike Collins and his girlfriend, Sherry. The afternoon had started out as a bit of a party. Garth and others were there, just drinking and chilling, but somehow, I didn't really register when suddenly people went outside to check out a horse.

Looking back now, I couldn't have set up Mike better. Not only did I not see a red flag that I was alone (it was likely planned that Mike sent people outside), but I gave him the perfect in to get me to test the cocaine. I had been complaining about the cocaine one of his relatives sold me on a previous trip, saying it wasn't pure and had been stepped on to make it weigh more. It was just a way to further build up my credibility. But it also gave Mike an easy opening to then say, "Well, this isn't. Have you tried this?"

The bag of white powder was in my face and the dog between my legs before I knew it. My heart rate increased, and I tried to control my breathing.

"Just taste it. If you're not a cop, just taste it!"

I protested as much as I possibly could that day. But I soon realized I was stuck and there was no way to talk my way out of this one. I was cursing to myself, wondering how I'd gotten into this spot.

The redbone growled.

Sherry looked on.

Mike sat there with his shotgun in reach.

"Just taste it!"

I responded, "Is this the test? Is this your test??"

I could have just said no, ordered him to move his damn dog, and walked out. But I chose to try a different tactic.

I wet my finger, put it in the bag, and did a little sleight of hand. "Are you fucking happy!?!? I can't believe I did this shit," I yelled, the anger coming to me naturally.

And just like that. Boom. The tension broke.

Mike became completely calm. Then he led me into a back room to check out his stash of drugs.

8

PILL SICK

Union County, Tennessee
2009–2011

The guys getting rich off the opioid trade were not your usual suspects. It took a few years until the Mexican cartels, the Outlaw motorcycle clubs, and street-level dealers fully grasped the extent of money being made from America's opioid epidemic, a.k.a. hillbilly heroin.

Big Pharma (in particular the Sackler family and Purdue Pharma) was the first to profit handsomely off the distribution of OxyContin once the powerful agent was approved by the Federal Drug Administration (FDA) in the mid-1990s. But a decade later, it was business tycoons and corrupt doctors and their staffs who made billions running pain clinics, which would issue bogus prescriptions for the powerful opioids.

Ground zero for these "pill mills" was Broward County, Florida. By 2009, there were more pain clinics than fast-food joints. The most famous dealers at the time were twin brothers Chris and Jeff George, who ran several clinics in the area and were eventually arrested and sentenced to more than two decades in prison following a massive joint FBI, DEA, and local police investigation.[1]

The opioid epidemic—which continues today—has been well covered in the years since, with articles, books, and documentaries exposing its roots and the cost for society. What I witnessed in the trenches during our Poetic Justice investigation was the sheer madness of what poverty and drugs could wreak on vulnerable communities. I saw up close what happened when those drugs from Broward County reached Union County.

The illegal pill trade worked like this: Carloads of users and dealers would make the thousand-mile drive from Tennessee to Florida and pose as patients with ailments that required pain medication. The obliging doctors would issue prescriptions with about the same level of care as a store clerk issuing a Powerball lottery ticket. Pharmacies, often right in the doctor's office, would charge about $5 per 30mg dose of oxycodone, which then could fetch at least $30 on the street.

Some of the popular pain clinics would make their clients park several blocks away in a waiting area so as not to draw attention with lines of "patients" snaking around their medical facility. They would then send a van for them to carry them to the clinic's front doors. These parking lots, where cars idled waiting for their turn, would become so packed that it wasn't uncommon to see what looked like drug-dealing tailgate parties.

The drugs would then come back and flood the rural Appalachian Region, which included Alabama, Kentucky, Ohio, West Virginia, and Tennessee.[2] Each state had a network of "sponsors," who would pay for the gas, office visit, and prescriptions in exchange for half of the scripts to sell on the streets, and in Union County we had many reports that local law enforcement was profiting off this trade.

I didn't fully understand what opioid addiction looked like until I met Mark Williams. Mark had befriended me near the beginning of our case, helping me sell illegal cigarettes, as did Mike Collins and a few others. I liked Mark and found him easy to talk to, and in the beginning, we got along just fine. But like so many others, he was addicted to pills and had a bit of a tumultuous homelife trying to support two little kids with his current wife and an older son from a previous relationship. To give you a sense just how crazy it was, his son confessed to me at one point that he had been sleeping with Mark's wife. "Your mother?" I asked. He looked at me like I was the crazy one, saying no, it was his *step*mother!

At one point during the investigation, Mark got locked up in Harlan County, Kentucky—which had nothing to do with our Poetic Justice case. He was picked up by local police on separate drug charges. When he was released, he came back to see me, and I'll never forget how he described his incarceration. Mark had been crushing about ten Oxy80s and fifteen to twenty Roxy30s *a day*. To put that in perspective, a doctor may prescribe one OxyContin 80mg tablet every twelve hours for pain, post-surgery. Mark's tolerance for opioids was so high, he was taking ten of those a day, on top of up to twenty 30mg pills of Roxicodone, another opioid.

When he got arrested, he was forced to go cold turkey and experience withdrawal on a prison-cell floor. It was hell. You name a physical symptom and Mark said he had experienced it: full-blown seizures, vomiting, diarrhea, fever, unbearable pain. If he could have found a way to kill himself, he would have. He couldn't eat for twelve days. It's amazing he survived.

One of the prison officials told him that in that year alone, in Harlan County, Kentucky, more than five hundred kids under the age of twenty had died from overdoses.[3] That seemed to really affect him. He said he didn't blame the cops for locking him up because they had lost a "whole generation" to drugs.

When he was talking to me, clean, he seemed determined that the experience made him stronger, and he saw the harm drugs had not only done to himself but to the community. "I ain't ever doing that again," he told me, vowing that his life now was all about his wife and kids. I looked at him and I remember my exact words: "Don't get back on the shit."

Two weeks later, he was completely strung out again and breaking into the back of my truck to steal cigarettes.

—

Undercover work can get pretty lonely at times. You never really get used to it. On Poetic Justice, though, I was lucky enough to have another agent working with me, who I introduced to the targets not long after I had ingratiated myself. He was a good friend of mine and continues to be today—I'll call him "Trucker Paul."

Trucker Paul joined the case because I needed to show I could transport my goods. As my legend grew, it wasn't just cigarettes I was dealing, but other "stolen" goods, including iPads, electronics, and generators.

On Operation Roadkill, there were agents who posed as truck drivers for specific stings, but Trucker Paul, who had his CDL (commercial driver's license), was considered a "secondary" on the case. That meant he often stayed in town with me. And he personally got to know the targets, including Mike Collins and Bonesy. Apparently, I wasn't the only one the dog didn't like—it seemed anyone who sat on Mike's couch would have the growling redbone in his crotch. I remember telling Trucker Paul the first time it happened, "Don't . . . make . . . any sudden movements!"

There were other undercovers who assisted, but Paul was there the most and I can't stress enough how much he helped me mentally.

After I'd underestimated Mike Collins that day in his trailer, we put in a request to FBI Headquarters to rent a proper cover home in the area that I could use as a secure base of operations. Up until then, for the first few months on the case, I'd been living in cramped cabins, usually so cold and small that I'd have to bring a portable heater into the bathroom and get on my knees to fit in the shower.

It was a little comical moving the paperwork past the lawyers and bureaucrats at headquarters who wanted me to produce a rental contract for the new place. The landlord, who I would give cash every month, owned a tire store in town. Our deal wasn't much more than a handshake.

Having that house was a relief, and it became a hub of activity at times. Trucker Paul, who was Cajun from South Louisiana, became famous for making huge batches of homemade chicken and sausage jambalaya when he stayed with me. To say it was great would be a gross understatement. I've been to top restaurants in New Orleans and tried jambalaya all over the South, and nothing comes even close to his.

But trying to better control my environment wasn't the only challenge on this case. I also had to try to control the rumors. And there was a lot of talk, and a lot of suspicion about the Marlboro Man, who was suddenly part of what is otherwise a pretty tight-knit community. Most of the time, as I had learned early in my career, suspicion can be overcome if there's money to be had. *Greed wins.* But I still did my best to try to mitigate what I could.

Gerald Bible, a local dealer who lived in a junkyard home guarded by two very angry chained pit bulls, was one of the persistent doubters. I got word that he was going to confront me, and I wasn't going to have an encounter like I did in the Outlaws clubhouse basement again. So when he came over to my new place to buy some cigarettes, I decided to switch the script.

I let him in and shut the door. We stood there for a moment sizing each other up. Then I told him that I couldn't be too careful and was worried *he* might be a snitch or a fed and I wanted to check for a wire. He needed to strip naked, I said to him, to prove he was trustworthy. He stood there stone-faced and, I'm sure, pretty surprised. Just to show him I wasn't wearing a wire either, I stripped down too.

Bible did as instructed, and we stood there for another brief second, naked, before we put our clothes back on and finished the deal.

But it wasn't just Bible who suspected me, so I needed additional ways to build my cover. But I can't disclose what I did without revealing tradecraft, as those same tactics may still be in use today.

The last precautions I took were the most important. Poetic Justice was the first major deep undercover case I had worked this close to home, which came with some pros and cons. The best part was being able to be there if Kara needed me. I could just tell my targets there was an emergency from one of my truckers slinging stolen goods in South Carolina, or whatever excuse I came up with, and bam, I was out the door and home in forty-five minutes.

But of course, working in your own backyard could be a problem, too. With my look and demeanor, I'm easy to remember. What if I was spotted by one of my targets with my family? Garth had reassured me when joining the case that our targets never came to the city, and I believed him, until one of the targets casually mentioned that he had been installing windows earlier that day.

Me: "Where were you?"
Guy: "Yah, I was down on . . ."

I won't name the street, but it was right by my house.

We had always been careful, but this was a reminder that we could never let our guard down. We didn't want anyone coming to the house and spotting our family photos—no unknown maintenance workers would be allowed in for sure. And we almost never went out in public as a family.

But there was one thing I wasn't willing to give up—worshipping on Sundays. My faith was central to me, and my family, and I had sacrificed that part of my life while working in McAllen on the Outlaws case. Part of making sure I could cope with the stress of the undercover job was being able to fulfill my duties as a Christ follower. For me, that meant playing guitar and singing for our church services on Sundays. The only problem was that our service not only would be viewed by the thousands in attendance but would also be live broadcast online and beamed to all our satellite locations and prisons. As one precaution, I did make sure the camera crew never captured my face. So, for approximately one and a half years, while I was working Poetic Justice, I would only appear as the "headless guitar man."

But what if I saw one of our targets in person at our church? I tried to prepare myself in advance for this scenario and imagined it would go something like this: I would just talk to them first as a Christ follower. I would ask them if they needed anything, or I could help with anything. Then we'd go outside, and I'd say, "Okay, what's going to happen now?" And I'd take it from there, hoping I could get them on board to help with the case. I mean, what better place to have a come-to-Jesus meeting than at church?

I was of course extra careful with my girls, too, and didn't go out with them in public as much as I would have liked to. I even tried to get them to use code words, or call me "Uncle," rather than "Daddy," which they could never quite get.

I remember on one of my daughter's birthdays, we had a small family party at the Build-A-Bear workshop in the mall. Remember those stores that had made-to-order teddy bears? I didn't want to miss it, so I went to the parking lot after Kara had taken the girls in, and sat for twenty minutes, watching. Then I went into the mall alone, trying to look casual as I meandered around, checking out all the other shoppers. When I was satisfied I hadn't been spotted, and hadn't seen any of our targets, I slipped into the Build-A-Bear shop and slid up to my kid.

Happy Birthday!

There are few things a good cop hates more than a dirty cop.

Based on the reports we were getting, our investigation wasn't into just one or two bad apples. Poetic Justice was a public corruption investigation—in other words, we were trying to build a case proving systemic illegal activity by law enforcement. We wanted to take down all the local law enforcement who wore the badge not to uphold the law, but to shield themselves from it.

But one of the challenges in our case was that the deputies and officers we were targeting with the Sheriff's Department and local police division all grew up in Union County. That meant there was a good chance they were related to some of the local criminals, or at the very least had friends who were. And it also distorted their perspectives on the law. When going to cockfights is as much a part of your childhood as river fishing was of mine, it is hard to suddenly flip the switch and crack down on the illegal gatherings.

I remember going to one cockfight with Garth early in the investigation and seeing more than one marked cruiser in the parking lot. Not only were the deputies and cops in uniform and turning a blind eye to the betting on murderous birds in the pit, but there were also plenty of pills and cocaine being traded right there in the open as law enforcement looked on. Ironically, I remember trying to get a beer but being told that was illegal. I thought to myself, *That's the law they're going to uphold?*

One of our targets was a forty-year-old cop named Dylan DeVault, a.k.a. Dyla, who was married to one of Mike Collins's daughters. Dyla had the stereotypical look of someone in law enforcement—close-cropped dark hair, prominent eyebrows, square jaw, and a thick neck. When we started the case in 2009, he was a reserve deputy with the Sheriff's Office who had no problem buying illegal cigarettes from me, selling me pain pills, or having the occasional snort of cocaine. By October 2010, he had been hired by the University of Tennessee Police Department and stopped openly doing coke, but he continued to buy cases of my illegal cigarettes and didn't mind showing up at my house in uniform.

On one deal, he pulled his cruiser up beside my truck and blared the car radio. Instead of talking, he wrote on a napkin his order for 115 cartons. I brought him the illegal cigarettes and he gave me about $5,400.[4] The second he left, I made sure to record every part of the deal in my daily investigative report, my "302."

Trucker Paul's jambalaya often brought Dyla and other officers to my house. I remember one day I had stepped out of the kitchen when Dyla said to Trucker Paul, "I need to ask you something serious." *Here we go*, Paul thought as he readied himself to face an interrogation about how long he'd known me, how we met, and anything else that could cast doubt on our cover story. Dyla continued to look serious and then said, "Can you give me the recipe for your jambalaya?" I told you it was good!

Another familiar law enforcement face at our place was John "Moon" Hubbs. Moon was about fifty years old, a Union County constable, and after Mark Willams introduced us, he took to me like a moth to a flame. He was so brazen in his dealing that one day when we were at Union County High School for the sheriff's reelection benefit, Moon summoned me to the bathroom to sell me some cocaine.

He loved to talk about all the cops he knew and what criminal activity they were up to, including allegations that someone in the Sheriff's Office was the grand wizard of the local Ku Klux Klan. He also made promises about how he and other cops could help me with my criminal activity. I knew Moon was our way in, but we had to move slowly and subtly. Unfortunately, Moon was not a subtle guy.

Garth was an endless source of unbelievable stories and our guide into this dark, sad underbelly of addiction. During one debriefing session, he sat in the front seat of my truck as a new female agent I was helping train listened from the back. She wasn't yet accustomed to my world and looked on with alarm as shirtless Garth told us about "Johnny Two Fingers."

Johnny Two Fingers?

In his matter-of-fact manner, Garth explained in his low, gravelly voice how Johnny got his nickname by having sex with his donkey. I continued listening, mirroring his nonchalance but noticing in the rearview mirror how uncomfortable the new agent was becoming. "I guess the donkey didn't like it," Garth said, describing how he turned suddenly and snapped off two of Johnny's fingers.

And everybody knows?

And he knows that everybody knows?

And he still lives here?

The answer to all three of my questions was *yes*.

Believe it or not, that wasn't even his most disgusting story of the day.

Garth also told us about a party where he had been with various deputies and cops and a seemingly endless supply of pills and coke. In the kitchen, he said, he watched a German shepherd have sex with a woman on her hands and knees. She was undoubtedly strung out, but not so much so that she wasn't saying, "ow, ow, ow."

"They pulled the dog off," Garth said.

But the story wasn't done. They pulled the dog off, he said, only to put socks on his front paws because she said it was the dog's claws on her back that was hurting. "So you didn't stop said sexual act?" I asked in disbelief. "You helped further said sexual act?!?"

I looked back at the new agent, and asked, "You getting all this?" She was now wide-eyed and nodding her head as she took notes, just saying, "Uh-huh. Uh-huh. Uh-huh."

Garth sometimes had a complicated homelife, and that complicated our case. His phone was constantly ringing with calls from his wife or kids as we were driving around setting up our deals. His ringtone became the soundtrack to our case.

Whoa, Black Betty, Bam-ba-lam.

He'd answer. "Yes. No. I told you I'm working. Love you. Bye!"

A few minutes later:

Whoa, Black Betty, Bam-ba-lam.

Garth's face would go crimson-red like some Chris Farley character on *Saturday Night Live.*

"WHAT?" (It would be a different kid.) "I told you Daddy's working. Love you! Bye!!!"

About three days later, after I had begged Garth to change his ringtone, off it went again.

Da . . . Da Da Da . . . Da Da DA . . . He had chosen AC/DC's "Back in Black" as his next phone ditty. "DADDY'S WORKING . . ." I'm not sure what ringtone was better. Both great songs, but after several days and hundreds of calls . . .

Garth was our main source but his whole family was part of the case. Garth had been with his wife for years, and they had grown up together. There was no way I could come on the scene as this new friend she had never heard of, and not raise her suspicions. That meant she knew my true identity, as did his older children.

One of Garth's sons struggled with addiction and had spent time behind bars. Unfortunately, on more than one occasion he tried to barter with me for money or drugs and threatened to blow my cover if I didn't agree. I don't blame him—he was a desperate kid, and to him, I was a golden opportunity. But in a practical sense, it meant I spent a lot of my time playing Dr. Phil, and not only making sure Garth was on the right track but also counseling his family. I remember once taking his youngest son, who was a pretty good athlete, to a sports store to buy some football equipment out of my own pocket. Helmet, shoulder pads, cleats, kneepads, pants—I knew how much I had learned from playing sports and I just wanted the same for him.

But sometimes the pressure for Garth just became too much. I remember one evening in early January 2011 as our case was nearing the end, he came to me at his lowest, and I really worried he was suicidal. I told him to hang with me and offered my place to crash, if he needed a break for the night. We stopped by the local gas station to rent a movie and get some beer. I picked up *The Wrestler*, the Mickey Rourke movie about an aging professional wrestler who kept going, despite his declining health and fame, and tried to find romance with a stripper, played by Marisa Tomei.

By the end of the movie, Garth was somehow recharged and, comically, I felt depressed. The night had cheered him up, and he decided to head back home with renewed energy to deal with whatever domestic woes he would face.

After he left, I kept thinking about the character Mickey Rourke played. *You can't stay young forever.* It was getting harder and harder for me to do the job.

Each undercover case I investigated over the years immersed me in a world most people would only see in the movies, and introduced me to characters that fully embodied the saying that fact is stranger than fiction. In Operation Roadkill, the Outlaws had a code, and lived by a set of rules, no matter how warped they may have been. But our targets in Union County? There was no one I could trust, and nothing they said could be taken as truth.

I used to love it when Mike Collins would tell me he had stopped using cocaine. "Scott," he'd say. "I used to do a ton of it, but I don't do it anymore. See this right here? It's just a bump." And he proceeded to snort the cocaine off his hand. He also professed to be out of the dealing business. "I used to sell truckloads of it, but I don't anymore," he'd say. Then he'd add, "But if you need those four eight balls, I can get them to you for $750!" Confusing, right?

We had one target who came to my house and poured cocaine on my kitchen island, prepping it to snort. I remember looking at Trucker Paul in disbelief and then yelling, "Hey! What the fuck are you doing? There are kids that eat off that island!"

"My bad," he said and shrugged.

When drugs run your world, your world becomes a starkly different place. I'll never forget one trailer I visited with Garth to buy pills. There were many dogs running around, feces and urine everywhere. The dealer, along with his wife holding a newborn baby, walked around barefoot. It took everything in me not to jeopardize the investigation by calling Child Protective Services and Animal Control.

In the end, two factors led us to wrap up the case. The first was Moon's arrest. After numerous conversations, buying drugs from him, and paying him bribes, Moon was setting up a meeting between me and other law enforcement officials he claimed were also dirty. However, when Moon contacted them, he painted himself as such a big player, they got suspicious. So much so, one of them contacted the Tennessee Bureau of Investigation to see if they were running a sting operation. When Moon went to the meeting, he was arrested for attempting to bribe law enforcement. I can't say for sure they were dirty, but Moon wasn't our only source saying they were. I remember the local paper laying out the entire scenario Moon had told the reportedly dirty cops. Supposedly, he never told them my name, but he did say that there was a person moving stolen goods and drugs through Union County that needed protection from law enforcement. It wasn't the exact scenario, but close enough.

It was a setback for sure, but we still had Dyla. I continued to make bribe payments and sell stolen goods to him. Dyla was already telling me which law enforcement officers from the Union County Sheriff's Office and Maynardville Police Department were willing to help me and which ones weren't. Although this was progress, it was tough knowing that I could be arrested at any moment because of the Moon situation.

The second factor concerned the Safeguard unit. More than a year into the case, the Safeguard team found out about the cocaine "test" Mike Collins had given me in his trailer. They opined that I should have notified them when it happened. But I countered that since I didn't ingest the cocaine and the case carried on, there wasn't any negative impact on my psyche. I also pointed out that there was no policy stating that I had to notify Safeguard in such an incident.

Well . . . it was policy now. At the conclusion of Poetic Justice, I was DNR'd (Do Not Recommend) again. Time-out number two.

I remember telling the Safeguard counselor, "For a guy who hates drama as much as I do, I sure find myself in it a lot."

He immediately responded, "Elvis wouldn't be Elvis."

"What the heck is that supposed to mean?" I asked.

He explained that without all the drama around Elvis, he would just be another guy.

So I decided I just needed to embrace it.

On Tuesday, May 24, the first thirty-four defendants were arrested, including Mike Collins and his girlfriend, Sherry; Gerald Bible; and law enforcement officials Moon and Dylan DeVault. In total, we would convict fifty-one dealers from an area with a population of just over two hundred thousand. It was a success, but stopped short of the sweeping police corruption convictions we had hoped for.

I remember sitting down with Mike Collins after he was arrested, and he said to me something undercover agents often hear at the end of a case: "Aw, hell, I knew you was the law the whole time."

"Yeah? Then why'd you sell me coke for over a year?" I asked.

"Oh," Mike said. "That's 'cause I like you."

After the takedown, I would receive voice messages from Mike on my undercover phone. “Hey buddy. It’s your boy Mike. I just wanted you to know I love you and I know you were just doing your job.”

I remember years later when a coworker sent me a link to an obituary. It was for Mike. He had died suddenly at the age of sixty-one. I guess it didn’t surprise me knowing the life he led. But I couldn't help but feel sad.[5]

9

I RECKON I GOT A LITTLE BIT OF HATRED

Myrtle Beach, South Carolina
January 12, 2017

Benji McDowell sat fidgeting in the back seat of my rental sedan, looking anxious and excited at the same time. He had doughy cheeks, a goatee, and a buzz cut, and even though he was twenty-nine years old, I suspect he got ID'd at bars when ordering a beer.

Benji was also a convicted felon. He had been recently released from a South Carolina prison, covered in white supremacist tattoos, and seven days earlier had posted this on Facebook: "Dylann roof did what these tattoos wearing so badass is supposed to be doing they don't give fuck about their white race. All they wanna do is stay loaded on drugs the Jews put here to destroy white man and they feast on the drugs. they should be Feasting on the enemy that stole their Heritage and their bloodline and trying to run us off of this Earth you can post pictures of fucking Viking and swords all the shit you want to post if you ain't got the heart to fight for Yahweh like dylann roof did you need to shut the fucking up damn right I'm pissed off when I see a fucking white young and disable beat him to death before fucking n****** and white people running: their fucking mouth not doing nothing!!!!!!! damn right I'm pissed off."[1] (Although of course he spelled out the n-word.)

A day later, Benji went searching online for an "iron," a.k.a. a gun.

His online activity wasn't the only red flag. The FBI's Columbia Division in South Carolina had received other reports about Benji and opened an investigation, putting out a canvass for an undercover agent.

Benji's praise of Dylann Roof was of course chilling. Two days earlier, in a unanimous verdict, the unrepentant Roof had been sentenced to death by a federal jury for his massacre.

The FBI later admitted that flaws in the federal gun background check system had allowed Roof to buy the .45-caliber handgun he used in the attack, when he should have been denied due to a prior drug conviction.[2] "I believe the job of the FBI Director is to be as transparent as possible with the American people, because we work for them. As you know, I try hard to explain our work to them, and I am also committed to explaining to them when we make a mistake and what I intend to do about it. I'm here today to talk to you about a mistake, in a matter of heartbreaking importance to all of us. Dylann Roof, the alleged killer of so many innocent people at the Emanuel AME church, should not have been allowed to purchase the gun he allegedly used that evening," then FBI director James Comey said in a statement following the killings.[3]

Roof's Facebook page also contained subtle symbols of white supremacy that were not flagged by his friends or family before the killings. In one photo, Roof was wearing a black jacket with two now defunct flags—one from apartheid-era South Africa and the other from Rhodesia, when it had a militarized white rulership, before becoming Zimbabwe in 1980.

Roof's physical appearance shocked many when he was arrested after the killings. He did not fit the profile of what we picture as a mass murderer. As journalist Rachel Kaadzi Ghansah wrote in a *GQ* magazine profile of Roof, he looked like a "young, demented monk." Roof's bowl haircut later became cultishly popular among violent white supremacists, one group even called themselves the "Bowl Gang" or the "Bowl Patrol."[4]

So the fact that Benji didn't appear very educated from his Facebook posts, and didn't look particularly menacing as he sat in the back of my car, meant nothing.

My backstory on the case, my legend, was that I was a longtime member of the cause—the "cause" being white supremacy. I had arranged to pick Benji up from his house in Conway, South Carolina, that January afternoon, and the plan was to take him to my hotel room in Myrtle Beach, so we would have some privacy to discuss his plans.

Benji was reported to us by members of the white supremacy movement. Take that sentence in for a second. Longtime members of the white supremacy movement thought this guy, Benji, was *too radical.*

But so far Benji hadn't broken any laws. His racist and anti-Semitic rants on Facebook, even though violent, were generally protected under the First Amendment—the right to free speech. My job was to figure out what he was planning and stop him before he could act.

Unlike my other undercover roles, where I was usually jovial, easy-to-talk-to Scott, I had a bit of a different persona when I did this type of work, which I called a "closer." If I was posing as a weapons dealer or a murder-for-hire thug, I didn't need to build rapport or be the target's friend—that would seem odd.

I kept an eye on Benji in the rearview mirror as we made small talk for the hour-long ride to my hotel. An acquaintance of Benji's sat in the front, beside me. About halfway there, I noticed that he had rolled himself a joint and was getting ready to fire it up in the car. I know marijuana isn't a big deal these days, but back then in South Carolina, it was a criminal offense, and I did not want this case to get complicated.

"Benji, let me ask you something about South Carolina," I said, my voice stern, steady, and low.

"All right," he answered.

"Is weed legal here?"

"No sir," he said.

"All right . . . I'm passing a shitload of cops, so I don't know where you're carrying that shit, but I can't be caught with it."

"All right, that's fine. I'll swallow that motherfucker," he answered.

"Okay. All right."

"It ain't nothing but a good blunt, sir."

"I can't be messing with none of that shit, I got too much at stake. You know what I'm saying?"

"Yes sir," he said. "I respect that 100 percent."

I must have made my point, because true to his word, he ate it.

When we got to the parking lot of my hotel, a Hampton Inn in a touristy area of Myrtle Beach, South Carolina, Benji proceeded to get out of the car and puke.

The summer before Benji's case, in 2016, I had decided to join the FBI's JTTF, the Joint Terrorism Task Force. The move wasn't motivated by a desire to work on terrorism investigations as much as, let's just say, an inability to see eye to eye with my supervisors. I always prided myself on being able to get along—that was part of my skill set. But there definitely were exceptions, and quite simply, I had been miserable working under my management in Knoxville.

My method as a case agent had always been to be a "producer," and strive to be above average when it came to running sources and investigations. That way, management wouldn't have a reason to tell me I couldn't take on additional undercover jobs and training, what we call "collateral duties." That worked for my entire career until early 2016, when all my requests were being denied by my supervisor and his supervisor.

I'd learned through time at the Bureau that good supervisors come and go. Bad supervisors come and go. These guys would not go, so I had to.

I went to the SAC (special agent in charge) to let him know I was stepping down from my collateral duties, and he asked me why.

"You know why," I told him, and said it had been getting progressively worse in the last two years. The SAC asked, if he moved me, where would I want to go? I thought that my experience would be a good fit for the JTTF, so that's what I requested. My SAC had me moved in about a week and a half.

The first major investigation I was involved with targeted members of the Aryan Nation, the largest prison gang in Tennessee. They often get confused with the Aryan Nations (with an "s"), so let me explain the difference.

Aryan Nations has a long history in the U.S. and was founded by American Richard Butler. Butler's inspiration came from two men he met while living in California after World War II: William Porter Gale, a retired army colonel who had been on staff with General Douglas MacArthur and introduced Butler to a racist, anti-Semitic, militia-type anti-government movement, and Wesley Smith, a pastor who preached dual-seedline theory.

That perverse theory, which is adopted by followers of "Christian Identity" (not to be confused with Christianity), goes like this: In the Garden of Eden, Adam and Eve had an offspring, named Abel. He went on to sire the white, European race. Then, as it is traditionally told in the Bible, Eve ate the forbidden fruit offered by a snake. But in the warped storytelling of Christian Identity, Eve also sleeps with the snake, who is actually Satan, and she gives birth to Cain. From Cain came the "mud people," meaning Jews and non-whites.

By the end of the 1970s, Butler had been ordained as a Christian Identity reverend and moved to Hayden Lake, Idaho, where he formed the Church of Jesus Christ Christian at his farmhouse. He named the political arm of his movement the Aryan Nations. The group had its heyday in the 1980s and early 1990s, holding an annual world congress at Butler's compound and inviting a gathering of neo-Nazis, skinheads, and Klansmen.[5]

But the Aryan Nation (no "s") is the Tennessee prison gang created by a guy who went by the street name "Legion." I met him in prison once, and he told me the group was affiliated with Butler's organization, but when it was first formed, they had no formal ties. Apparently Butler had been so incensed by the prison group using his group's name, he actually sent cease and desist letters to Legion. Legion said he told Butler he wasn't changing the name because people had already bled for the group.

In the end, they negotiated a deal. Butler agreed the Aryan Nation could keep its name if members agreed to learn and follow the practices of Christian Identity. And that's what happened.

When in prison, Aryan Nation felons have certain rituals—like carrying a rock that signifies their membership, or attending "church," and reciting the well-known "14 words" white supremacist slogan, created by David Lane, a member of the terrorist group known as The Order: "We must secure the existence of our people and a future for white children."

When not in prison, Aryan Nation members slipped into a pretty active crime syndicate (home invasions, robberies, drug distribution, prostitution). I had one member tell me, "We move into your town and wreak havoc."

I remember asking another member how pimping out the groups' women—the Aryan Angels—was working toward the cause of protecting the white race. (They needed to make money.) And did they only sleep with white men? (The answer was no.) It was pointless to get in these types of debates with white supremacists, about the hypocrisies in how they preached and acted, or their interpretations of the Bible or Norse mythology, but sometimes I couldn't resist.

For the Aryan Nation case to fall under JTTF, we had to show three factors: evidence of a federal crime being committed; use of violence; and an ideology or political motive. We couldn't target them simply because of the hate they espoused, because that is generally First Amendment protected. And we couldn't go after them for terrorism charges, because in the U.S. there are no federal domestic terrorism laws, only ones for international terrorism.

A good friend and coworker of mine, Mike Raleigh, had a case opened on a violent ranking member of the Aryan Nation. Numerous reports were coming in that he possessed multiple firearms—which is illegal for a felon. But *every* time we stopped him, wouldn't you know it, no weapons.

As the investigation progressed, we learned that several members of the Aryan Nation were slinging a lot of dope and committing various other crimes. As more and more investigations were initiated, we were able to show that profits from their criminal activity were used to further their violent extremism, which meant our Domestic Terrorism Operations Unit (DTOU) gave us the green light to continue. Later on in the case, we joined forces with the DEA, which had been working a separate investigation in Johnson City, Tennessee, that targeted the same suppliers.

About six months into the Aryan Nation investigation, I saw the canvas for the Benji McDowell case, and my new supervisor happily gave me permission to work on that at the same time.

Before I went to pick Benji up at his home, I checked into my hotel and set up my room so I could record our conversation. At one point as I headed back to the lobby, the hotel elevator stopped working and there

I was trapped, looking like a thug, beside a very nicely dressed, prim and proper woman. You could almost feel her fear fill the elevator as I was on the phone with the front desk trying to get us help. Can you say awkward? It might have been only thirty or so minutes, but it felt like hours. She stared straight forward, never looking in my direction. Then I remembered what a good undercover friend of mine said . . . Sometimes we forget how bad we look.

"Ma'am," I said. "I know I look pretty rough, but you have nothing to worry about. You have no idea how safe you are right now." When we were finally released from our temporary prison, I was able to score us both meal vouchers to our pick of restaurants for our troubles!

When I arrived with Benji later the next day, after he had puked in the parking lot, we made our way into the hotel room.

I remember our talk felt like one of the longest conversations in my life. The only clue of any plans we had was from a Facebook post and what our sources had told us. On December 26, 2016, a couple weeks before Benji started praising Dylann Roof, he wrote cryptically, "I love love to act what u think," and posted a link to a conservative synagogue in Myrtle Beach.

When I talk to targets, there's a red line that I can't cross—I can't put words in a suspect's mouth. That would be entrapment. Benji was a tough case because at first he wasn't sure what he wanted to do, he just passionately knew he wanted to do *something*.

During our conversation, I learned that he had found white supremacy while serving an eighteen-month sentence for burglary in a state prison. Unfortunately, this is a well-known problem. It's not uncommon for gangs to form in prisons along racial lines, and groups like the Aryan Nation have done most of their recruiting from inside U.S. correctional institutions.

When Benji was released, he found a chapter of the Ku Klux Klan and attended one of their rallies in Alabama, where his rhetoric was so violent, he spooked the other white supremacists.

Benji was upset about not being able to get a job because he was a convicted felon, he told me. I thought to myself—but didn't ask—how not getting a job at a corner store led to targeting a synagogue.

"I'm wanting to do this shit, and I got the heart to do this," Benji said as we recorded every word. "I seen what Dylann Roof did, and in my heart I reckon I got a little bit of hatred and I want to do that shit." I tried to just let him talk it out, nodding as if I understood. "I want something where I can say, 'I fucking did that' . . . me personally." He added, "If I could do something on a fucking big scale and write on the fucking building or whatever, 'In the spirit of Dylann Roof' . . ."

In an effort to slow his plans down—and buy us time—I suggested to Benji that maybe he should look somewhere other than his hometown, where he was a known felon. He had already said he did not want to get caught and go back to jail, and I just wondered aloud if because he was well known in the area it increased his risk.

I'm not the type of agent who thinks everyone is a ticking time bomb. I come into cases with an open mind and let the evidence take me where it takes me. But as I handed in my recording gear to the case team, I remember saying something like "I'm 99.9 percent sure that if I was really a bad guy and gave him instructions for an attack, he would carry it out." But I also felt confident that he trusted me, so if he was going to take the next step, he would contact me.

Turned out, I didn't have to wait long. As I sat at the hotel bar hours later, just killing time until my flight back to Tennessee the next morning, I got a message on my undercover phone. It was Benji.

I searched for a phone app that could record our conversation, since I'd already turned in all my equipment to the Myrtle Beach case team, and called him back.

"If it ain't too much trouble, you think I could get a .40 for me personally?" he asked.

Without missing a beat, I answered, "What you want? You want a Glock or—"

"It don't matter, just a .40," he interrupted, then added, "I don't know if right here would be good because I'm too famous."

It seemed my words about not attacking close to home had sunk in. We had time. And now we had a convicted felon trying to procure a weapon, which was something he could be charged with. We could get him off the streets and stop an attack on innocent people if we were successful. I didn't let myself think about what would happen if we lost him.

—

Two weeks after I first met Benji, I was on the phone again with him as he laid out more plans, although exactly what he was going to target and how was still unclear. "I just be plotting it out, like, I mean you just run up there on them if they back there partying, and all, with a fucking AK and rip them sumbitches down, and throw, a damn, something at them." We confirmed on that call that it would be a .40-caliber Glock that I would sell him. A couple weeks later, he called to make sure I could also bring hollow-point ammunition, which are bullets that expand upon impact, making them more lethal.

The case team then learned that Benji would soon be on the move. We didn't know where and didn't want to risk losing him, so we had to get going. I gave him a call to let him know I had his purchase, and we arranged to meet on February 15. He told me he'd be heading out of town—to Alabama. I offered to give him a ride as I was also heading that way for business.

I remember when I picked him up at his mother's home there was essentially a monsoon assaulting the area. Through the pounding rain we drove to his grandfather's house, where Benji picked up some money for the handgun and bullets. It was going to cost him $109.

On a conference call with the case team, planning for this day, one of the more inexperienced attorneys had said we would need to hand over a fully loaded, operational pistol in order to prosecute him. I immediately objected, not just as the undercover, who would be giving said handgun to Benji, but also as lead tactical instructor, and as a case agent who would never advise this.

In the end, we agreed we could give Benji a Glock that was inoperable, and if all went well, he'd be in custody before he even tried to use it.

With the windshield wipers whipping, I slowly drove my rented SUV along Celebrity Circle and eased into the Hampton Inn parking lot. I parked in a designated spot that we had predetermined would strategically help in making Benji's arrest.

Inside my hotel room I gave Benji the Glock and he shoved it into a red bag he was carrying that held little else except a marijuana joint and cellphone. We weren't there long. I packed up my bag and we headed back out into the parking lot to my SUV.

Seconds later the Task Force team swarmed.

"FBI! Let me see your hands! Don't move!"

They went for me, too, slamming my head against the cruiser in a way that sounded worse than it felt. I was handcuffed and put in the back of a car much too small for my frame. "Be cool!" I screamed to Benji. "Be cool!"

After I was let out of my cramped custody, and was back on the road to Tennessee, Benji confessed to everything. According to the case team, he said he was *glad* they caught him because he was really going to do something bad. So if there was ever any doubt about his motivation, there wasn't now. I was glad we caught him, too.

At his trial, in the summer of 2018, family members told the court they did not believe he was prejudiced and that he struggled with mental health issues. "He's no Dylann Roof," said Nancy Clewis, one of McDowell's grandmothers, according to a TV report. "He was raised up with Blacks, they are his friends, he's not no prejudice boy."[6]

U.S. District Judge Bryan Harwell ordered Benji to undergo mandatory drug testing, mental health counseling, and vocational training and sentenced him to thirty-three months in prison.

10

THE KLAN BAND

Scottsboro, Alabama
April 21, 2017

My night was not going well. I was driving around alone on a Friday evening, with no cell signal, trying to find the designated meeting spot. I had been invited to this in-the-middle-of-nowhere location a few weeks earlier by John Jack. (I'd later learn "Jack" was a nickname because of his passion for Jack Daniel's.)

Jack had been the voice on the other end of the line when I called the Ku Klux Klan hotline. It's really handy when the hate groups you want to infiltrate have a hotline.

I told Jack I got the number from a bunch of guys I was chatting up at the gas station. They were wearing leather cuts like the bikers did, but they told me they were with the Loyal White Nights, a Klan group popular in South Carolina. They mentioned an upcoming rally and told me to call the hotline to learn more.

I ended up talking with Jack for about forty-five minutes. I asked if the rally was maybe like the Bike Weeks I'd been to—you know, vendors, booths, beer, maybe some dancing and music? He said there *would* be vendors and food, but . . . he had a band lined up and the singer had just been locked up and he didn't know what he was going to do now.

It was my opening. Trying to sound as casual as possible, I asked him, "Did I mention that I'm a musician and a singer?"

"Tell you what I'll do, if you want," I offered. "I'll bring my PA system and my acoustic to your spring rally. I'll play something out by the car for you. If you think it sucks, I'll put it right back in the car, and I'll just hang out. But if you like it, I'll play."

Jack responded: "God dang, that's awesome, man."

But once I started running through my set list, I had to eliminate some of my favorite songs from some of my favorite artists, including Otis Redding, Ray Charles, Bill Withers, Prince, Hootie. Heck, even if there was a Black musician in the band, I took them out of the lineup. Then just when I thought I had my tabs ready to go, I saw I still had Jimi in there. *Shit!* So out went Mr. Hendrix.

As I drove around lost on that April night, I just sang to myself with my PA and guitar in the back seat until finally, *finally*, I saw a bunch of big guys with big weapons and leather vests guarding a gate and I knew I had arrived.

It's hard to imagine that in 2017, these types of Klan rallies still existed. But the Ku Klux Klan, America's oldest and most infamous hate group, is still very active. They have tried to rebrand themselves these days as not being "white supremacists," but rather simply "white separatists." The message is the same. I was once told by a Klan member, "We're not about white supremacy, we're about white separatism. Don't mix the races. You don't see dogs and cats fucking breeding . . . or horses fucking cows."

But the Klan has lost most of the influence they once had. According to the Southern Poverty Law Center, the number of KKK groups has declined steadily over the years due to infighting, which long has been the hallmark of the Klan. The organization is also slowly being replaced by newer racist and more militarized groups that continue to multiply across the country and appeal to younger recruits.[1]

Those who belong to the Klan openly despise anyone who is not white, or is Jewish, and in more recent years, anyone who identifies by any sexual orientation other than heterosexual. But those views, however despicable, are protected by the First Amendment and don't break any laws. So, like the Aryan Nation case, where I was a case agent (and was still actively investigating) in 2017, we once again had to show there was illegal activity furthering their cause in order for us to investigate the Klan under the umbrella of the JTTF.

The case, which we called "Smoking Robes," was opened because one of the FBI's field offices in Alabama had received reports of illegal gun activity among the members of the Klan that Benji McDowell had met, reports such as convicted felons possessing weapons, or the presence of ghost guns, which are constructed at home, often using 3D printers. They don't have serial numbers, making them untraceable.

The rally checkpoint was guarded by the Knighthawks, the Klan's militarized security detail who wear ceremonial black robes and hoods, instead of white. As I got closer, I immediately recognized some of them from their mug shots I had studied. But even though I was looking at a crime right there—felons illegally possessing weapons—I knew the USAO (United States Attorney's Office) would need more for an airtight charge, such as being able to prove they were real firearms.

"How you doin'?" one of the Knighthawks said.

"Good! Took me a while to find it! I . . ."

"Who are you?" he answered, not in the mood for my chitchat about the drive.

Walking into a bar where I didn't know anyone for an undercover investigation? No problem. But rolling up alone to a checkpoint of Klan members after having talked to one person on the phone was awkward to say the least. I sure hoped I wouldn't have to call on my "quick response rescue team" from the local division, which consisted of a white female agent and three Black male agents. Their arrival would definitely be noted.

I lowered my voice. "Scott. John Jack knows I'm coming. He said when I got here to tell you guys and y'all would radio for him."

The Knighthawk grabbed his radio. "Hey, John, you got Scott up here at the front gate."

We waited. He repeated the radio call. It crackled to life.

"Go on in, turn up there, and you'll see a tent on the left."

As I drove up, the stage came into view—where I hopefully would be playing later that evening. I also saw a solid metal cross, wrapped in burlap and half propped up, that must have been twenty, maybe even thirty, feet tall.

I found Jack, and he eased me into the gathering, immediately acting as my guide as he laid out all that would happen during the rally, including how the burlap would be soaked in diesel. (I had learned that diesel was nicknamed "Klan Kologne," since it's impossible not to get a little on you when you stand the cross up.)

"Now, Scott," Jack said. "It's not burning a cross that would be sacrilegious. It's a cross-*lighting*."

"The reason we light the cross is to take out the darkness of the world and bring in the light of Jesus Christ." He told me he had seen guys bigger than me watch the cross-lighting ceremony and wiping away tears because the ceremony was that beautiful.

Jack also let me know he was the "Kludd," which is the Klan chaplain, and told me about the Knighthawks, who were "strapped with ARs and AKs" and providing security.

"I'm not gonna bullshit you. I only have one guy in South Carolina," he said. "We're trying to build South Carolina. If you don't have a problem with that, I don't have a problem with that . . . I'll have you naturalized tonight."

I quickly answered, "Sure."

Then I walked closer to him as those around us walked off, and asked, "Hey, Jack. What exactly is a naturalization anyway?"

"We do a little thing. You get blindfolded. You might hear a gun go off." He said naturalization was like *The Wizard of Oz*. It starts out black and white and ends in color. A whole different world.

—

The imperial wizard began his speech.

He spoke for ten minutes, until it was time for the naturalization ceremony. I felt like I had to go along—if I didn't participate, I would be the only nonmember there not taking part in this ceremony.

"I'm like Bob Barker," the imperial wizard shouted to start the ceremony, chuckling to himself at his joke. "Come on down."

I stood with the other new Klan recruits waiting for our instructions. The guy in front of me had a bad leg and easily had a decade on me, maybe even two. "Even if we both fall, you just fall on top of me," I said to him, adding, "but I might pee on you, because I've been holding it for a little bit—if you fall on me." We laughed, trying to break the tension as they blindfolded us. It all felt a bit farcical and menacing at the same time.

"Does anybody here have any guns on them? There will be no guns!" someone yelled.

I tried to look out of my blindfold, but I couldn't see shit. Plus, it was getting dark.

"Hold the right shoulder of the person in front of you and do not break the chain!" a new voice thundered out of the darkness.

Then one of the Knighthawks was given permission to speak. He talked about "immigrating" to the "racial community" of the United Klans of America and becoming "loyal citizens of the South." Then collectively we had to answer ten questions with a yes or no, the first question being: "Are you a white, gentile, American citizen?"

As they instructed us to march through a field, a dog joined us, and I could feel his hot breath and hear his panting. When we ascended a hill, I found myself holding the man in front of me up by his right shoulder because his bad leg was giving out and he was close to falling.

"It has come to our attention that there's a snitch in the group!" someone yelled.

Then there was a loud BANG.

Normally, I'd have been worried. But Jack had given me a heads-up that at some point in the ceremony they would try to scare the new members.

"And you know what happens to snitches," the voice continued.

BANG, BANG, BANG.

Suddenly the sound of gunfire filled the field. We stood there, still all blindfolded, hanging on to each other. The gun show went on for a while before it went quiet again.

"Raise your right hand," came a voice.

I didn't do it, and continued to hang on until the voice came closer, and closer and closer, until it was almost right in my ear, and I could feel his breath on my cheek.

"Raise your right hand!"

"But . . ." I said in my best squeaky Pee-wee Herman voice, "he said not to break the chain . . ."

There was a pause. "Uh, it's okay, raise your right hand."

I raised my right hand.

"I do swear from this moment forward to fe . . . festering my . . .

FOSTERING the welfare of the white race and further the work of America's greatest movement, the United Klans of America . . ."

I had to bite my lip a few times during the ceremony. Of course, I'm not making light of this hateful exercise, but the ritual made me think of a scene from *Django Unchained.* There were times when whoever was reading the script would mess it up and another voice would chime in to correct him. They'd backtrack and start again. It would have been hilarious if it hadn't been so sinister.

We were told to kneel and then one by one our blindfolds were removed. I blinked into the darkness, seeing Jack in his green Kludd robe with a sword of some sort. He touched the blade on my shoulders as if he were knighting me. "Congratulations," he said. And then people started hugging.

In the pitch-black darkness I walked back to my car to get my gear so I could finally start playing. I went through what had just happened, starting to worry about the FBI bureaucracy and the questions I might get asked.

Did I have the right approvals for that ceremony?

What exactly happened?

That's when it hit me.

I think I just joined the damn Klan.

Yep, I just joined the Klan.

—

On the night of August 11, America woke up to what I was already starting to see in my domestic terrorism undercover work.

That Friday evening, about one hundred white supremacists, white nationalists, and neo-Nazis marched, carrying tiki torches, on the University of Virginia campus in Charlottesville, Virginia. Some gave the Nazi salute as they chanted slogans that included "white lives matter," and "Jews will not replace us."

The shocking march was followed the next day by a larger "Unite the Right" rally protesting the removal of a statue of Confederate general Robert E. Lee, considered a symbol of white power. During the march, white supremacist James Fields Jr. drove his car into a crowd of counter-protesters, fatally striking thirty-two-year-old Heather Heyer.

Sometimes it takes a tragic incident like that to swing the pendulum in law enforcement. I'm not saying we didn't investigate white supremacist groups—I had personal experience in many cases, and we were still pursuing the Aryan Nation investigation. But after the September 11, 2001, attacks, a good majority of the resources on the national security side of the house, and definitely most of the public attention, was focused on international terrorism. Charlottesville changed that. Domestic terrorism was now front and center.

At the time, I was still undercover in the Smoking Robes case, and being taught about our country's racism by current Klan elders. Every Wednesday night, I would attend "Klan Kraft Klass," for new members, in a private Facebook Messenger group, studying "The Basic Klansman Handbook," "The Kloran," and learning their constitution and bylaws. I learned code words like "LOTIE," which refers to women in the Klan as "Ladies of the Invisible Empire." Or that the original MIOAK (Mystic Insignia of a Klansman) has "K's" arranged in a square facing outward to form a cross-like shape. The "Klass" prepared us for the "K-Uno" test, and if we passed, we could get fitted for our hood and robe.

I continued to gather intel on the group and attended their summer and fall rallies, before the case fell apart. I can't go into the details about what happened, but there were issues with both the source and the case agent, and in the end, I was out of the undercover operation. As far as I know, the investigation ended without any arrests.

The Aryan Nation investigation, however, was a huge success.

On the morning of January 9, 2018, teams spread out across Tennessee to make the arrests in a case that brought in nearly a dozen local police and sheriff's departments, along with the FBI and DEA. In total, there were forty-four individuals charged in a meth distribution ring.[2]

Since I was the case agent on the investigation, I sat in our command post, overseeing the arrests taking place in the Knoxville area. Our teams presumed anyone could be armed and ready to use their weapons. Just a few days later, a thirty-one-year-old well-known Aryan Nation member, who wasn't part of our investigation, opened fire on a Knoxville police officer when he tried to stop him for speeding.[3]

The arrests went off without incident: Strap, Red, Fingers, Ellie Mae, Junior, J Dawg, Shoe Guy, Bearded Mike, Mohawk, Dee Dee, Tattoo, Lil' Bro, Boston . . . the indictment lists all their street names.

While the charges may not have mentioned terrorism—since no such federal offenses exist—numerous defendants were part of violent white supremacist organizations, including the Aryan Nation, the Aryan Brotherhood, the Dirty White Boys, and the Ghost Face Gangsters. For the next while anyway, they would be off the streets.

11

I KNOW A GUY

March 16, 2018
Greenville, South Carolina

Travis Dale Brady was an angry white guy who was fired from his job at the Michelin plant in Greenville, the city where I was born. In 2017, the FBI's South Carolina Columbia Division opened an investigation, after they got a tip that he wanted someone to pay for his termination. Murderous revenge. The case was still going after we wrapped up the Benji McDowell case in early 2018, and I went home to Tennessee.

I hadn't been back long before the supervisor of the Columbia Division domestic terrorism squad called to see if I was interested in returning to South Carolina. After some failed attempts, they had another chance to go after Brady due to a new, well-placed source.

This would be one of the more standard murder-for-hire jobs I'd worked on. You'd be amazed how many times there are canvasses for this type of undercover role as a contract killer. Many of the cases are not that sophisticated, and those looking to murder someone aren't always geniuses with their OPSEC (operational security). But it doesn't matter. Dumb people manage to kill people all the time.

There was also a racial element to the case, and having just arrested Benji, this type of hate crime was still very much on my mind. Brady had originally wanted to blow up the Michelin plant after he lost his job, but he eventually decided he would target and kill two of his colleagues, a Black couple he blamed for his firing. Brady hated the couple and was known to refer to them as "animals."

These investigations are generally short term, and over in just a few meets—similar to a "closer" position. And it wouldn't be the first time I had posed as an assassin.

—

One of my cases was in Tennessee, in January 2015, and I was brought in as a killer-for-hire over a $90,000 insurance policy. The suspect was a man named Michael Keller, who had been having an affair with Aleshia Stuart, and together they plotted to kill Stuart's husband to receive his insurance payout. Through a source, Keller had agreed to meet me in Dandridge, Tennessee, to discuss the murder.[1]

But when he rolled up to the Econo Lodge motel in an old truck with a rebuilt title, I let him know there was no way I'd take that worthless vehicle as collateral. It was a bit of a gamble, but I didn't think I'd look credible taking such a low guarantee.

To my surprise, he then said that Stuart had also offered her gemstone ring toward collateral if the truck title wasn't enough. I happily agreed to the new deal. When he came back, not only did he have the ring, but Stuart was also in the truck with him. We arrested them both as they walked up to the hotel room.

After he was in custody, I remember introducing myself as Scott

Payne, FBI agent. Keller sat there on the hotel bed looking worn out, breathing hard. He told me he was actually relieved I was FBI. He had never hired a killer before and was terrified that the person I was pretending to be would kill him.

Two days after they were arrested, Stuart's husband, Randall, filed for divorce.[2]

One of the first contract killer investigations I worked was also one of my most satisfying undercover cases. It was in Texas back in 2004, and we were following a tip the FBI San Antonio Division had, reporting that an inmate named Raymond Jackson was looking to have someone killed.

The details were chilling. Jackson was on trial for sexually molesting a minor and trying desperately to get released by targeting the victim in his case.

I went to the county jail where he was being held before his trial and walked into the visitors' room. There was a bank of phones, each stall separated by stainless steel, and I remember the noise of the room—baby mamas and relatives yelling and crying, their voices echoing and bouncing off the walls. I needed our conversation recorded and struggled to hear what Jackson was telling me. Not exactly easy. It was also hard to hide my utter disgust, but luckily, that's not a bad look for a supposed contract killer.

Jackson had been told my name was "John Lewis," but we hadn't yet built an undercover profile for that name. Thankfully, we had a well-trusted sergeant working at the jail who "checked" my ID, to grant me access to the visitors' room, where Jackson confirmed he had been expecting me. "You know I'm in the extermination business, right? I get rid of pests," I continued, in not-too-hard code to decipher. I then showed him a photo of who he told me he wanted killed and asked if I had the right "bug."

Jackson confirmed, clear as day on the recording: "That's him."

We agreed on a price to conduct the murder and it wasn't much, just like the wife-boyfriend murder case in Tennessee. Those $100,000 contracts you hear about in the movies aren't exactly what you find in the real world. I've seen some, but they are rare.

Jackson wanted me to act quickly because he had heard the target was moving and then he might not be able to find him. One more time I asked him if I had the right target. "Are you sure this is the right bug?" He immediately said "Yes."

We continued to talk in low voices, straining to hear and be heard over the noise of the room. I asked how he wanted the "extermination" done. Did he want it to look like an accident, or did he just want him gone? Jackson replied, "Whatever is the easiest." Then he added, "I would like the whole family gone."

I couldn't believe his level of depravity. I replied, "Well, that will cost more money. I'm not against traveling, but let's deal with one pest at a time."

Before my next—and final—visit to him in jail, I stopped by the San Antonio Solicitor's Office in Bexar County. All the attorneys in the Crimes Against Children Unit happened to be women, and when I walked in, they all stood up and began clapping. This set me back a bit. I was humbled. "Well, thank you, ladies," I said. "But for what?"

They explained that they had been after this guy for *years*—but he had walked on four previous molestation charges. Maybe that's why he had been so bold in hiring me. Did he think he was above the law? Or was he desperate and terrified of being convicted because he knew pedophiles did not do well in prison?

Jackson ended up pleading guilty to both the murder-for-hire charge and the sexual assault. He got thirty years. Good luck.

But if the case against the pedophile at the start of my work was the most satisfying, well, the one that I did in Ohio, just before my retirement, may have been one of the most dark and bizarre.

When the case was concluded in 2020, as COVID-19 was sweeping its way through America and around the world, Muskingum County Sheriff

Matt Lutz sat before journalists, wearing a black cloth face mask, his hands folded before a stack of papers and a pink highlighter, to deliver the news of the convictions. He seemed unable to believe the facts of the case himself.

"This might be some type of thing you'd think you might see on television and here it is in little Zanesville, Ohio," he said in announcing the indictments of Michael Shane Siegenthal; his wife, Tami Siegenthal Bailey; and her thirty-year-old son, Brett Bailey. They were facing a myriad of felonies that included: conspiracy to commit murder, conspiracy to aggravated robbery, and conspiracy to aggravated burglary. Mike also got an extra drug possession charge for possession of methamphetamines.

I had known Tami for weeks leading up to her arrest, during the summer of 2020, right after I had had my second painful spinal lumbar fusion. At first, she hired me to do some home invasions—her son ran dope for dealers in the area, and he knew where the guns, ammo, drugs, and money were in each target's house. But it didn't take long for our talk to turn from theft to murder.

She believed I was a one percenter biker and hitman—alongside an FBI Task Force officer friend of mine.

Tami, who was inching close to fifty, had been living hard. She wore tiny jean shorts, hunting boots that came up to her knees, and most days she couldn't stop scratching her skin. I've met a lot of drug users, seen dark things, but I never had conversations like the ones I had with Tami. "If you need someone tortured, I like torture," she casually said one day as we were driving around on a tour of all the local drug dealers' houses.

Then she went on to describe some of the things you could do to someone. One tactic involved sticking the bent end of a hanger up a man's penis and then jerking it out. *Fast.* Follow that by pouring salt in the wound. *Literally.* (It's worth noting here that as I recovered from the lumbar operation, I'd had a dry catheter post-surgery.) As Tami described this, I could hear my undercover colleague, who was sitting in the back of the truck, say, "Oooohhh damn . . ." She also talked about inserting a PVC pipe up an anus, followed by barbed wire, which once again would be ripped back out.

At this point I was near the end of my career, and I remember thinking as Tami was talking, *These are my people . . . this is where my skill set leads me.*

When Tami bragged to us about how she stapled her husband's scrotum to a two-by-four because he had been on a three-day coke binge, I'll never forget what my partner asked her.

"Hmm. You really don't like men a whole lot, do you?" my TFO (Task Force Officer) colleague asked.

Tami replied, "I have been unlucky in love."

As I pulled up to a red light, I leaned over to Tami and asked, "Do you watch a lot of slasher flicks?" Her response . . . "Yes. That's all I watch."

In the end, Mike was given a sentence of ten years behind bars, but Tami got eighteen. Brady, her son, got two years. The assistant prosecutor on the case, John Litle, told the court: "She is the most responsible person in this conspiracy, and she minimizes and does not take responsibility for her acts." At his sentencing, Mike said he didn't want to rob or kill local drug dealers but feared his wife.

"All it would have taken was a phone call," Judge Mark Fleegle told him.

Mike replied: "I was scared."[3]

—

My first interaction with Travis Brady about his plan to kill his Black former colleagues was by text. He was too scared to talk on the phone, so he insisted on only texting. We started out vague, as I tried to assess what he was looking for.

Then . . . if you can believe it . . . he sent a KABOOM emoji. So much for being cautious. Evidently, he was filled with so much hatred toward the couple that he couldn't help himself. Soon, we were texting about what explosives I could get him, what their potential blast radius was, and other logistics.

Then I asked him to specify exactly who he wanted to kill. Brady clearly wasn't too worried anymore because he sent me the Trulia listings—the actual real estate details—of the couple he wanted dead.

Our FBI bomb technicians constructed a fake explosive. The bomb—as requested by Brady—would be designed to explode when the victims opened the package it was in . . . KABOOM. Just like his emoji.

The day I was supposed to meet him to deliver the package, however, did not go quite according to plan. Instead, I drove around all day with an inert bomb in my car, trying to contact him, playing phone tag. I kept thinking, *Knowing my luck, the cover team will lose me, and I'll get pulled over by law enforcement, with a dog, who will hit on the C4 in my car.*

But the following day we got the package delivered to him successfully. And once the case team had the evidence to show that he was mailing the fake bomb to the couple, they moved in and made the arrest.

Brady ended up getting ten years in a federal prison.

These murder-for-hire cases helped me to build on my skill set of convincing people that I really was a bad guy. And they helped me to act quickly on the fly, and as the cliché goes, expect the unexpected. These targets also taught me a lot about humanity—or lack thereof. It is incredible how little respect some people have for life.

At their core, though, most of these cases were about drugs, money, revenge, or sometimes a combination of all three. For most of my career, those factors drove the majority of my investigations.

But the investigations into Benji McDowell, the Klan, Travis Brady, and others had shifted my undercover work to focus on a different type of crime; an ideological one, driven by the hatred of someone's skin color, politics, or religion. It's harder to crawl into the heads of these types of criminals and be among them—to mirror their hate. We can all understand addictions, greed, and spite. But this type of criminality is about a deeply held belief system that's foreign to me.

Domestic terrorism was definitely on the FBI's agenda since the Charlottesville "Unite the Right" rally, and there were dozens of agents running cases both with the Bureau and other law enforcement agencies. But this neo-Nazi movement we were tracking was growing quickly in numbers and sophistication. In particular, there was a new breed of "accelerationists" who were organizing, training, and plotting violent acts in the hopes of sparking a race war.

By the summer of 2019, I would find myself in the deep end of that pool of hate.

As a beat cop with the Greenville County Sheriff's Office.

Standing in my favorite gas station to consult my "fashion advisors" for my undercover work.

"Orders" night at FBI training in Quantico, Virginia. I was just about to find out that I was headed to New York City, which I had picked as my 36th choice out of 56 possible field offices.

Photo with my daughter as I played Santa. I was trying to use a voice she hadn't heard before so she wouldn't realize it was me at our FBI Christmas party.

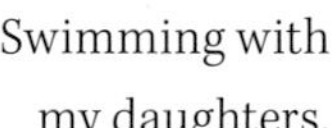

Swimming with my daughters.

Playing at Sunday service at my church. My faith has always been central to who I am. After I had my crash in 2006, I made sure to keep my church and faith community close.

A surveillance shot from 2006 outside of "Lobsterfest" Brockton, Massachusetts with the Outlaws, as part of "Operation Roadkill." *Nancy Morelli*

A photo taken on the Outlaws case during the "drug protection" operation. The cocaine and marijuana would be transferred from one truck to another.

The flag of the Outlaws, the main biker rival to the Hells Angels and the group I infiltrated for nearly two years.

A Ku Klux Klan rally in Scottsboro, Alabama on April 21, 2017, where I went undercover to play in the "Klan band," as part of our "Smoking Robes" investigation.

A photo of Base propaganda circulated to all members, taken during a regional training camp in August 2019. The photo was submitted as an exhibit in the District of Maryland Court case against Patrik Jordan Mathews and Brian Mark Lemley Jr. Lemley is second from the left, holding a long gun straight in the air. William Garfield Bilbrough, another Base member I befriended, is kneeling holding the knife.

A photo of me after I had passed the face-to-face vetting process with The Base and was given one of their trademark balaclavas and patch with runes (which is on my mouth). *Nathan Plough*

A recruiting poster for The Base, a neo-Nazi accelerationist group I infiltrated in 2019.

The Base runes and hate symbols that we carved into wood and then bled on as part of our "hate" blot or worship ceremony.

A photo I took of one of the Bibles that the Base members tried to burn. When the Bible wouldn't burn, I considered it to be divine intervention on a crazy night.

Standing at my retirement party with Knox County Mayor Glenn Jacobs, who had long been a hero of mine for his skill as the wrestler "Kane." *Mitchell Bain*

A session I taught on domestic terrorism at a July 2023 conference in Mississippi, after my retirement.

I retired from the FBI in the summer of 2021.

On stage with my co-author, Michelle Shephard, at the "Eradicate Hate Global Summit" conference in Pittsburgh on September 20, 2022.

12

SAVE YOUR RACE, JOIN THE BASE

Rome, Georgia
July–August 2019

In twenty-five years of undercover work that I have done, I have never had to burn Bibles, or set fire to an American flag. I've damn sure never been with a group of people who stole a goat and sacrificed it at a pagan ritual, then drank its blood.

I did all that over just three days with "The Base."

—

My path to becoming an undercover Nazi began online.

I was in Phoenix, Arizona, helping instruct an FBI course at a time when violent far-right white supremacist groups were proliferating across the U.S. and on everyone's mind. Not only was the FBI worried about these organizations, but our international partners had been contacting us each time they started investigating these groups in their own countries.

One of the most active organizations at the time was an accelerationist group that called itself "Attomwaffen Division" (AWD). AWD's mission was to bring about the collapse of society, in the hopes it would spark a race war. Members had initially found each other on an online fascist forum named Iron March, which began in 2011 and was active until it closed down in the fall of 2017. Attomwaffen, which is the German word for atomic weapons, wanted to create small, terroristic cells and were among the first new wave of accelerationists. The Base, which aimed to be a type of umbrella group under which accelerationists, including AWD, could come together, came next. Some members said they belonged to both groups.[1]

The training I was doing in Phoenix was with a good friend of mine from Ohio, the same task force officer who worked with me on the Tami Siegenthal murder-for-hire case. He was especially skilled at online undercover investigations into radical extremists, and I remember saying to him, "What're your plans tonight?" and he replied something like "I was going to get dinner with everyone."

"How about this," I said. "Let's hit the liquor store, swing through a drive-thru, grab our laptops and phones, and meet up by the firepit at the hotel. If you're good with it, I need you to coach me and help me create a persona online."

We stayed up drinking until the late evening, bringing my online undercover persona to life. I was posing as a National Socialist looking for a white ethnostate and posting horrific Holocaust images, among other memes and photos. A "National Socialist" is what neo-Nazis call themselves. When I teach courses on domestic terrorism, and in particular white supremacism, this is the definition I give: Since Hitler believed that ethnic and linguistic diversity had weakened the fortunes of Germany, he saw democracy as a corrosive force, because it placed power in the hands of ethnic minorities, who he claimed had further "weakened and destabilized" the success of his people. Simply put, in order for Germany to be "strong again," it needed to be made up of a master race, a pure Aryan people who had not been polluted by outside forces and insidious immigrants.

Well, National Socialists don't last long on Facebook, which they refer to as "Jewbook." Getting kicked off can be a badge of honor. But no matter how hard I tried at first with my racist and horrific posts, I wasn't getting canceled. I confess I was not a Facebook guy before this case, so I asked for help from one of my amazing undercover colleagues, who was also an instructor. She *nicely* pointed out, "Scott . . . you don't have any friends." So I added some friends from "People You May Know." *Click click click* . . . and I was banned.

Next, I joined the social media app Gab, and started reaching out on chat groups such as "Whites Only" or "14 Words" (which is the reference to the white supremacist slogan coined by David Lane).

I also created an email account under an alias, and reached out directly to The Base, which had provided an email address on their Gab account. The Klan had a phone hotline, so I guess it made sense that the next generation of white supremacists were trying to recruit by email.

My first email on July 15, 2019, was short and direct: "I've been seeing your stuff and I'm definitely interested," I wrote. "Survival and self-defense . . . I like it."

Things moved relatively quickly after that. The next day, on June 16, I got a reply: *Ping.*

"Thanks for contacting The Base. You can learn more about us on our official Gab account: @The_Base (it's new because our account was recently banned for the fourth time). If you're interested in joining, please provide the following info to begin the vetting process:

Name (pseudonym is acceptable)
Age (approximate is acceptable)
Sex
Race
Location (country & region)
Military Experience
Physical Fitness Level
Science or Engineering Training
Org Affiliation (past & present)"

"I'm liking the scrutiny," I wrote back a day later. "That shows you have a standard. Here's my info." I told them I was in my forties, didn't have military experience, but my fitness level was high. For past affiliations, I listed the Hammerskins, a white supremacist group that started in the late eighties in Texas and were big into white power rock music. I also wrote that I hung with some members of the White Knights, the Klan group from South Carolina, and other motorcycle clubs.

By our third or fourth email that week, they were asking if I was willing to travel as far as Rome, Georgia, for meetups, noting that they had a cell there. "Also, I want you to know that the age range of members is heavily skewed to 18–25. There are a couple members your age. Will this be an issue?" I told them both factors were fine. I'd be happy to travel, and in some groups, "I'm the old man, in others, I'm the young one."

I was actually forty-eight years old at the time, although I would later tell them "Scott Anderson," which was my undercover name for this investigation, was forty-four. I had made sure to memorize everything I needed to know about my legend, including the dates I might be asked to cite—such as date of birth or graduation from high school (which would be four years later than my actual dates).

I also knew there *were* a few older members in the group. One in particular: the elusive founder of The Base, who went by the online names "Norman Spear" and "Roman Wolf."

He was actually the first member I talked to. I found out later, Roman Wolf was the one answering my email.

—

The public became aware of The Base after *Vice* published an exposé by journalists Ben Makuch and Mack Lamoureux on November 20, 2018. The headline read "Neo-Nazis Are Organizing Secretive Paramilitary Training Across America."[2]

"A Neo-Nazi who goes by the alias Norman Spear has launched a project to unify online fascists and link that vast coalition of individuals into a network training new soldiers for a so-called forthcoming 'race war,'" the story stated. "Spear, who claims to be an Iraq and Afghan war veteran, is a self-proclaimed white nationalist with a significant online following. His latest act involves bringing Neo-Nazis together, regardless of affiliation and ideology, into a militant fascist umbrella organization. His tool for doing this? A social network he calls 'The Base,' which is already organizing across the U.S and abroad, specifically geared toward partaking in terrorism."

The FBI had been investigating the group, and in particular Norman Spear / Roman Wolf, around that time. Especially concerning was a ten-acre block of undeveloped land that he bought in December 2018 near Spokane, Washington, where he was allegedly going to hold a training camp for The Base. But his plans were exposed by an Oregon-based anti-fascist group known as "Eugene Antifa," which alerted the local media and law enforcement.[3]

We knew Roman Wolf's real identity. He was an American citizen, born in New Jersey, in his mid-forties, and as the *Vice* story noted, he had done time in Iraq as a contractor for the U.S. Department of Justice. His real name was Rinaldo Nazzaro, but that would not be publicly known until the *Guardian* and *BBC* outed him in January 2020.[4]

I didn't have a lot of time to prepare for my first call with The Base—the invite to talk came after less than a week of emailing. One of the questions they had asked was whether I knew *Siege*, which is basically a bible / how-to book for these groups. "I ask because the general philosophy and outlook in *Siege* underlies The Base and our mission," the email stated.

James Mason, the book's author, is still alive, living out his neo-Nazi retirement in northern Colorado, denying any connection to the violence his book has sown, but defending what is essentially a call for far-right violent groups to stoke a race war. I hit up my buddy from Ohio to get a copy of the book and made sure to thumb through it before I got on the call, getting a fast education in the group's hateful verbiage. I was specifically looking for parts in the book I could easily remember and then portray as things I really admired from Mason's teachings.

I was at home in Tennessee on the sweltering hot and humid Friday in July when I was supposed to accept the call on an encrypted app called "Wire," which the email had instructed me to download. I was worried they might ask me to put my camera on, and do a 360 of my surroundings, so I decided to walk a little distance from my house into the woods. I cautioned Kara and the girls not to come looking for me or call my name.

With about fifteen minutes to go before the designated time, I was already sweating like crazy and second-guessing my decision to be outside in the woods. Then I looked down at my arm and it was completely black. It took me a second to realize it was covered in mosquitoes. *Screw this,* I thought, and ran back to my driveway and climbed into my old truck. I quickly cleared out anything personal, making it as sterile as possible, and drove to an empty movie theater parking lot. Then I waited.

—

Nazzaro, a.k.a. Roman Wolf, started the call saying it would last thirty minutes. But in the end, we talked for about an hour. There's no script for this type of work—you just have to believe you're who you say you are, and then figure out how that person would answer.

As always, I tried to stay as close to who I am as possible. I described my work as a bouncer, gave them my physical appearance, and said I'd hung around with bikers and the Klan (just omitted the essential fact that I did so as an undercover agent). I told Nazzaro that a buddy had suggested I check out Gab after I "kept getting banned from freaking Jewbook."

"I'm always looking for likeminded brothers, comrades, whatever you want to call it," I said. "Anything to further the white race and furthering that kind of brotherhood, but real." Then I mentioned that I had been around Klan groups I'd known were "just posers."

When Nazzaro asked me what I was looking for in The Base, I answered, "I'm looking for the fourteen words. I'm looking to secure the race, but I don't think you can do that by yourself."

A lot of the call was Nazzaro talking, trying to describe the organization—both what they supposedly were and what they weren't. He stressed more than once that it wasn't a political organization but more of a pragmatic, "down-to-earth" survivalist group, and what they were doing wasn't illegal.

"They may not like what we're doing," he said about law enforcement and the media, which he called "the enemy press." "They may not like what we stand for, but at the end of the day everything we're doing is within the laws."

Just as the call was wrapping up, he asked the others on the line if they had any other questions. I could detect three other voices, but there may have been more.

"If you were going to develop leadership qualities in somebody, how would you do it?" asked one member, going by the name Landser. It sounded like something you would get in an interview for a corporate position.

"First thing I'm gonna do is lead by example," I told them and then described two ways of mentoring. You could tear someone down and build them back up. Or you could instill a little confidence and support them.

Next from Landser: "Anything you're not willing to give up in the pursuit of victory?"

I described my "warrior mentality" and how I would set my mind to something and not stop until it was accomplished. If only they knew how I was applying that right then in my role as an undercover agent.

One of the last questions, again from Landser, was: "Do you think we should make use of useful idiots—i.e., like sending in the stupid ones for suicide missions?"

This time I couldn't contain my laugh. "Well hopefully you don't have a lot of idiots in the group." I wasn't sure what type of answer he was fishing for, so I opted for being a good team player and added, "If everybody decided that it was a good idea to send the idiot in, and we got one, well, you know . . ."

Nazzaro ended the call saying he liked to give everyone a twenty-four-hour grace period to think things over. It would give me time to think about The Base and whether I wanted to join, and give members the time to discuss what they thought of me.

True to his word, less than twenty-four hours later, I got a text on Wire from him.

Ping.

"We'd like to officially invite you to participate in The Base network. Let me know if you accept."

I replied quickly. "I consider it an honor and I'm looking forward to it."

Then I sent a screenshot of that message to all the case teams involved and FBI Headquarters.

—

Luke Austin Lane was just twenty years old when I met him in Rome, Georgia, in the summer of 2019, after I had passed the Wire interview, and he and Pestilence vetted me face-to-face for membership. Lane was the leader of the group's Georgia cell and went by the online name TMB, or "The Militant Buddhist." He may have been young and didn't look much like a tough guy, but I learned after that very first meeting, when he used that handheld wand to try to detect a tracker on my truck (which thankfully my team had turned off in time), that he knew what he was doing and was very careful with the group's security.

"Pestilence" was nineteen-year-old Jacob Kaderli. He had chosen his call sign because Pestilence was the name of one of the Four Horsemen of the Apocalypse. Like many teenage boys, he was full of piss and vinegar, and very self-assured. He was also a huge conspiracy theorist, believing Hitler was still alive.

After I passed their IRL (in real life) vetting on that stormy day in a cement plant in Rome, Georgia, I followed Lane and Kaderli back to Lane's farm, where The Base's Georgia cell would hold training camps. He lived on a one-hundred-acre property with his dad, his sister Brooke, and her husband and kid. His parents had divorced, and I never met his mother. Lane had been homeschooled by his dad and managed to hold down some stint jobs and earn enough wages to afford to build up his arsenal at his dad's farm.

Lane's dad, Tom, worked in construction and fiercely loved his son and daughter. It was that daughter, Lane's sister, who impressed me the most. She was in her mid-twenties, mother to a sweet three-year-old boy, and always wore a pistol on her hip.

Like Lane's dad, Lane's sister was not involved in The Base, which the members all tried to pass off as no more than a prepper survivalist group. If it *had* been simply about survival, then I'd have trusted Lane's sister more than any of the guys in the group. She'd kill a deer in the early morning and have it skinned before the guys even woke up for breakfast.

We had picked up some drinks at the liquor store in town on the way, and once we got to the barn, we settled in to get to know each other. There was an old house on the property, and the barn had been converted into a residence. All around there were trees and hills, creeks. It was really gorgeous—and incredibly private.

Kaderli was quizzing me on how to hold a rifle, and as I showed him, he said something like "That's so Boomer." Here I was the head tactical instructor for my FBI division, a seven-year member of the SWAT team, and Kaderli is not only correcting me but essentially calling me an old man?

The words in my head went something like *Who are you to tell me...*

But what I actually said was, "Oh. How do you hold it?"

We didn't actually train that day, just continued chatting. By the time I left, they had gifted me with a black balaclava, a signature for The Base, and a patch with their symbol of three Eihwaz runes, which were supposed to symbolize life, death, and rebirth.

Back at my hotel room that night I met with a case agent from Seattle who had flown into Georgia. The FBI's Seattle Division was where The Base case began, due to the property Nazzaro had purchased in Washington. But it was quickly drawing on more than a dozen of our divisions as suspected members were popping up all over the U.S. I put on my newly gifted balaclava, Velcroed the patch near my mouth, and gave a little thumbs-up, so the case agent could take a photo for the rest of the team.

Now I was fully a member, "patched in" as the bikers would say.

I changed my Wire handle to "Pale Horse."

—

The next day, I arrived back at Lane's farm and discovered that two more Base members had driven through the night to join us from the Baltimore, Maryland, area. They called themselves "Eisen" and "Cantgoback." Cantgoback was former U.S. Army and had done a tour in Iraq, so he knew how to hold a weapon. (Although that wouldn't stop Kaderli from later showing Cantgoback how to do it. Kaderli often believed his ways were better than what the military taught.)

Eisen's real name was William Garfield Bilbrough, and he was still a teenager and acted like one. He was a stocky, redheaded, 170-pound pizza delivery boy who lived with his grandmother and trained in mixed martial arts. Cantgoback was Brian Lemley, a truck driver in his early thirties. He owned some expensive guns and a very nice truck and was probably the most well-off financially in the group.

Most of our "training" that day involved firearms, and Kaderli was leading it. At first, I held back, not knowing if any of them knew what they were doing. But other than Bilbrough, they were all pretty skilled, which made me feel safer while I was there training, but even more worried about what they may be planning if they broke bad.

Lemley, a.k.a. Cantgoback, had a 6.5 Creedmoor, which is a sniper rifle. Surprisingly, I think that day was the first time I ever fired one, and I was impressed at how smooth it was, with such little kickback.

It was just the five of us training—Lemley and Bilbrough, representing The Base's Maryland cell, and Lane, Kaderli, and me as the Georgia cell. There was one other member from Georgia who I would later meet: Michael Helterbrand, who went by the name Helter Skelter until he changed it to Skelter Helter, because he thought it might keep people guessing about his identity.

Helterbrand was in his mid-twenties, held down a job as a computer specialist, and even had a girlfriend—which was rare in this group. He was not only determined, he was also well armed and had an unregistered AR-15 that he would bring to Lane's farm, among other weapons.

After my successful infiltration, I went back to Tennessee to keep working the case by phone. The Base's group chat on Wire was active—new members coming in and some leaving the group after they had been doxed (outed) by Antifa groups, or the media. Every time the identity of a member was publicized, the group would improve their OPSEC to try to avoid being infiltrated again.

"For all we know the feds could be monitoring everything we post everywhere on Wire," Nazzaro, a.k.a. Roman, wrote at one point. "Let's just continue to use common sense and we'll be fine."

One of the members in the chat used the call sign "Dave Arctorum," and he was from Canada. He had been busy trying to recruit new members in his hometown of Winnipeg, Manitoba, by putting up Base posters that read "Save Your Race. Join the Base." He got a couple hits, and managed to recruit a university student who joined our chat as "Mark."

But just two weeks later, on August 16, 2019, "Mark" published a front-page news article in the *Winnipeg Free Press* about the Canadian cell of The Base. "He stands about 5'10", with hair that's shaggy on top and clipped close at the sides. He pulls at his bushy beard when he's deep in thought. His arms are often crossed when he talks. If you walked past him on the sidewalk, you wouldn't look twice," wrote journalist Ryan Thorpe, a.k.a. Mark. "He wants to recruit young white men for a race war. He thinks one is coming and can't wait for it to get here. His group idolizes serial killers and mass shooters, referring to the likes of Oklahoma City bomber Timothy McVeigh and Charleston church shooter Dylann Roof as 'the saints.' His name is Patrick and he plans to establish a white supremacist terror cell in Manitoba."[5]

The Wire chat lit up.

"Boys I'm pretty shook here. He's literally describing me. Fuck," wrote

Dave Arctorum, who had introduced himself to the undercover journalist as "Patrick."

Ryan Thorpe had reached out to the group the same way I did, by their email. And he was also invited to meet in person for a face-to-face vetting. That's how he met Dave Arctorum in person and knew what he looked like. But when he was invited to become a Base member, the newspaper sensibly pulled him, and published their investigation.

"I almost got doxed," Dave Arctorum wrote, clearly distressed.

Roman wrote back right away, "But you didn't."

Cantgoback (Lemley) weighed in. "Bro if you actually retaliated id pick your ass up at the border and hide you forever. Pisses me off that we just have to absorb constant attack and just wait for the boogaloo. Because don't have media power to buttfuck someone as a weapon. [*sic*]"

Dave Arctorum wrote back, "Nah I'll just wear a wig and dress like a homeless guy lol then got him, no witnesses he got attacked by a homlesser. Happens all the time. [*sic*]"

But then, less than twenty-four hours later, the *Winnipeg Free Press* wrote a follow-up story after Thorpe got a tip as to who "Dave Arctorum" really was.

His name was Patrik Mathews and he was a reservist in the Canadian Army. The story was huge and went viral after the RCMP raided Mathews's home and took him in for questioning. He was later released and wasn't charged, but his photo was all over the news.

I figured maybe the attention would make him leave the group. Instead, Mathews just changed his name on our Wire group to "Jimmy the Frog Rancher," and wrote about being outed. "I'm dead to mom and my dad hates The Base," he wrote. "He thinks you guys threw me out like a piece of meat. The opposite is true, remember to anyone here that this joint is full of dead set legends who have your back." That text, and others like it, were so telling. There was a brotherhood among these young men; a desperate need to be appreciated and accepted and be a part of something bigger than themselves. It was a toxic mix of insecurity and bravado. "Just remember," Mathews wrote, "doxing isn't the worst thing. They shot Codreanu and left him in a ditch. It can always be worse."

Corneliu Zelea Codreanu was a violent anti-Semite and leader of the main Romanian fascist organization known as the "Iron Guard," which was formed in the 1920s. His image had been revered by neo-Nazis in recent years, such as Matt Heimbach, a twentysomething popular white supremacist who wore a shirt emblazoned with Codreanu's face at the 2017 Charlotteville rally. A year before, a video of Heimbach violently shoving a Black woman protesting U.S. president Donald Trump went viral. Heimbach made no attempts to hide his extremism—having his picture taken unfurling a Confederate flag at Rev. Martin Luther King Jr.'s grave site or standing at the U.S. Holocaust Memorial Museum in Washington with a sign that said: "6 million? More like 271,301."[6]

Soon after Mathews sent that text, Lane (who was calling himself "Mr. K" in this Wire group) removed him from the group, writing only, "Will explain soon."

I didn't give Mathews a whole lot of thought after that, as I had my hands full with the Georgia crew. But then the Canadian media reported that he had disappeared. His abandoned red Dodge pickup was found on a rural property in Sprague, Manitoba, near the U.S. border.[7]

13

HATE CAMPS

Silver Creek, Georgia
August–October 2019

I used to love to go camping with my parents and friends. When I was growing up in Greenville, South Carolina, we lived next to a river that had miles and miles of woods nearby. It was heaven for a country kid. I'd spend my summers fishing and exploring with my buddies, or by myself.

In my early teens, I started developing the work ethic that I still have today. I get it honestly from both my parents. My mom would work up to eighty hours a week, but that wouldn't stop her from driving more than three hours on the weekend to watch my college football games, whether I was playing or not. Then she'd stay, take me and my friends out for food and a couple of drinks, before making the drive back along Highway 26. She admitted she would sometimes feel the vibration on the edge of the road, which would thankfully wake her up.

My father may not have completed high school, but he built a very successful landscaping company, and would put me on jobsites with his crews. I knew that these grown men, who poured whiskey in their coffee and smoked filterless cigarettes, would be looking at me as a spoiled daddy's boy. Respect was not given. It had to be earned. So I did everything I could to outwork them. I wouldn't rest. Or I would say something like "You know, we'd get a lot more work done if you didn't take so many smoke breaks."

Fast-forward now to me in 2019. As I inched toward my fiftieth birthday, I was working around the clock trying to build a case against The Base, which included planning camping trips with a bunch of aspiring white supremacists half my age. I could never have imagined when I was young that this was where life would take me.

My friend Terry Rankhorn once described undercover work like playing a game of chess. Terry worked at the FBI for nearly two decades, along with his wife, and like me, he was a certified undercover agent and taught at the Bureau's Undercover School. "There's a lot of common misconception about undercovers . . . that they're used car salesmen," he'd say. "They're slick talkers, all of this. And that's really not the case. They're strategists. They're playing a game of chess. And you have to understand the consequences of pushing your queen out in the middle of the board."[1]

Playing chess with The Base was never easy. White supremacy has a long history in the U.S., but this new accelerationist movement was still relatively unknown and unpredictable. I wasn't the only undercover agent working these types of cases in the U.S. And I was constantly sharing information with other agents and bureaus.

Groups like The Base were devised to be "leaderless," even though the founder, Nazzaro, seemed to exert a lot of power. Around the time he founded the group, Nazzaro moved to St. Petersburg with his Russian wife and their children. *New York* magazine ran glamorous photos of their 2012 wedding in a feature called "The Prep School Nazi." The story began: "*Six years before he would found a neo-Nazi group called the Base—Mein Kampf–ing its launch with a tweeted Hitler photo and the caption 'Führer, you were only the beginning. We will finish what you started'—the prep-school grad from New Jersey was getting dressed in his room at the Standard Hotel in the Meatpacking District. His father, Michael, helped him into his tuxedo jacket. Playing the best-man role, his friend Don fastened a white lily to the lapel. Later, he would be known to his followers as Norman Spear. Now, at 39, he was just Rinaldo Nazzaro. An earlier engagement hadn't worked out, but today he was getting married.*"[2]

I suspected from the hours of the day that Nazzaro was sending me messages, over an encrypted email server called Proton Mail, that he was in Russia. While I was undercover in The Base, I remember him coming to the U.S. once, but I didn't get to meet him. He visited relatives in New Jersey and Arizona on that trip and met other Base members near the Northeast, handing out to cell leaders knives inscribed with the group's name.

After *Vice*'s article about The Base, the media started picking up stories, and Antifa (anti-fascist) activists were working all-out to dox as many Base members as they could. On September 10, 2019, less than two months after I had infiltrated the group, Congress's Committee on Homeland Security started to hear testimony on this new threat.

"Thank you, Chairman Thompson, Ranking Member Rogers, distinguished Members. Thank you for hearing my statement today," began Ali Soufan, an American former FBI special agent, who had been born in Lebanon and was involved in several high-profile terrorism cases after the 9/11 attacks. "Tomorrow marks 18 years since al-Qaeda murdered nearly 3,000 people on American soil. As we honor the dead, we remember too the importance of remaining vigilant. Today I draw four main conclusions: First, both al-Qaeda and the so-called Islamic State remain potent threats; second, in addition to the jihadi challenge, we now face clear danger from white supremacist extremism; third, there are important similarities between these two groups of extremists; but fourth, under its current approach, the U.S. Government is at a clear disadvantage when it comes to combating white supremacy.

"Al-Qaeda," Soufan told the committee, translates to "The Base."

Soufan went on to compare the mistakes we made before 9/11 and what we were doing wrong now in handling white supremacy terrorism. He noted that in 2018, white supremacists had killed three times as many Americans as Islamists. But still, only transnational groups like Al Qaeda were given federal terrorism status, which allowed us important investigative tools for monitoring suspects and also the ability to charge someone with a terrorism offense. "We need to recognize the international nature of this threat and start treating white supremacist terrorists the way we treat other global terrorists," Soufan told the Committee.[3]

There were a lot of similarities between the way Al Qaeda and The Base organized and the propaganda they developed. I remember after 9/11, the videos of Al Qaeda's training camps in Afghanistan that played over and over on the news; jihadis in masks and holding AK-47 assault rifles as they fought and trained.

Now, nearly two decades later, here I was, posing as Pale Horse, staying up all night texting with Base members asking to attend their "hate camp" to train and make similar propaganda.

After that first two-day meetup in August on Luke Lane's farm, our communication moved online to our Wire group chat. It wasn't just one group chat—there were several—and sometimes I would also be DMing with individual members. It was a full-time job. My daughters were in their late teens at the time, but unlike a lot of teenagers, they were pretty good about not spending too much time with their heads down on their phones. We all made sure to always put the phones away for meals or time together. I was probably the busiest, by necessity. But if I caught myself never looking up, I would make sure to put the phone down for a period, or step away if the matter was urgent.

Every night, I would go through my phone and take photo after photo of all the texts that were sent, as evidence. The group's texting was so fast, sometimes there would be dozens and dozens of frame grabs to record.

In mid-September, Landser started to post regularly about "Operation Kristallnacht." Kristallnacht, which means "broken glass" in German, was the name of murderous Nazi riots over two days in November 1938. During the rampage, thirty thousand Jewish men were rounded up and taken to concentration camps, marking the first time Nazi officials arrested Jews with no other purported justification than on the basis of their religion.[4]

Landser was enraged over the doxing of a South African Base member and wanted us to act. "For far too long have 'we,' the inheritors of the National Socialist Revolution, sat on our hands and waited for 'someone else' to do the heavy lifting for us," Landser wrote in our Wire chat. "How many brothers have been doxed? How many have been killed? Too many, far too many—The time has come for us to act with the tenacity and ruthlessness of all our fallen Comrades. Know that they are marching with us in spirit, always, eternally." He told us that we should revolt between September 20 and 30, hitting any non-white-owned businesses or churches, slicing tires, smashing windows, and tagging synagogues with graffiti.

"You, as a revolutionary, will be expected to strike at the vulnerable lemmings, traitors, and their Jewish puppet master. Smash the glass, slash the tires, leave the symbol of our revolution wherever you go, and burn whatever you please." His message continued, trying to rouse the group into action, writing in caps, "VICTORY or MARTYRDOM."

One of the members, who went by "Joseph" online, replied, "Sieg Heil."

A beat later, Lemley wrote, "Well that escalated quickly. Sieg Heil."

Landser added that Antifa was the main enemy, but this operation would be about going after the "low level threats like n****** and commies."

"I daydream about killing so much that I frequently walk in the wront [*sic*] directions for extended periods of time at work," Lemley replied.

I stayed quiet on the chats, letting it all play out, taking photos of the texts.

A few days later, on September 21, a synagogue in Michigan was hit, vandalized with swastikas. The next day, another synagogue, this one in Wisconsin, was tagged with anti-Semitic graffiti.[5]

Landser turned out to be an eighteen-year-old from New Jersey named Richard Tobin, and he was a member of not only The Base but also Attomwaffen Division. I remember being on group calls with more than a hundred FBI case agents, supervisors, and lawyers debating what we should do with him. That's how big this case had grown, with agents spread out across the U.S. following up leads and opening investigations on various members. There was considerable public outcry over the anti-Semitic vandalism. But internally at the FBI, we had concerns about arresting Tobin, or others. Could it hurt the other cases we were still investigating? Did we know what else was being planned? These are the types of debates you often have on long cases, and I remember being asked if I believed we had "full coverage" of Base activities with me on the inside of the organization. My answer was simply "No." I knew that there were side chats among different Base cells, or direct messaging between members, that we weren't seeing.

A month later, FBI Special Agent Jason Novick, who was with the Joint Terrorism Task Force (JTTF) out of our FBI's South Jersey Resident Agency, interviewed Tobin. During questioning, Tobin admitted his role in directing others to vandalize as part of his "Operation Kristallnacht," telling them to "tag the shit" out of synagogues. He also told Agent Novick that he had considered "suicide by cop," and thought a suicide bombing would be pretty "bad ass."

Tobin also gave the names of the two other Base members who had vandalized the synagogues.

He was arrested in November.

The criminal complaint written by Novick said that "Tobin also stated he had saved manuals regarding how the detonation would work for the bombing, and he believed that it would be 'pretty straightforward' to fill the back of a truck with barrels like Timothy McVeigh did."[6]

—

Aside from continually monitoring the online chatter, I was making the three-and-a-half-hour drive back and forth from my home to Lane's farm in Silver Creek, Georgia, to attend as many of the get-togethers and training sessions as possible.

Lane was the main organizer in the Georgia cell. His texts were very specific about what we should bring when we trained and looked like this:

Sleeping bag
Tent (If you want a personal tent with privacy and don't want to cuddle with the bros in the big tent)
Hydration carrier or a case of bottled water
Rifle & Sidearm—Bring a sling and holster
Rifle ammo—at least 600rnds for rifle to participate but 1,200rnds are recommended just in case
Pistol ammo—at least 200rnds for sidearm to participate but 400rnds are recommended
Mags—6 rifle mags and 3 pistol mags
Food & Water—Bring your own food and drinks or have enough money to buy what you need, bring plenty of water none will be provided, and it'll be needed
Sunscreen—If you wear sunscreen bring your own

Changes of clothing—5 changes of clothing
Uniform—commoflage [*sic*] pants and jacket (preferably flecktarn) if you are unable to bring that bring a black T-shirt or long sleeve and black, green, or tan pants if possible
Ball cap or boonie hat
Boots—Good quality boots, preferably black

The lists would go on and on. I always made sure to book a hotel room—Pale Horse had no desire to cuddle with the bros at night. Around the end of August, Lane added a new member to our group chat who went by the moniker "Thomas Andersson." The next training camp I attended, Thomas led a "Blot," which was a pagan ritual reaching back to the time of the Vikings. The Blot was essentially a ceremony to honor the gods.

After the weapons training, which was standard at every camp, we went down into the woods and began the ceremony. Andersson said he was a member of a group known as the Asatru Folk Assembly and said he had led numerous Blots before. Kaderli, a.k.a. Pestilence, said he would assist. It was just Andersson, Lane, Kaderli, and me. Helterbrand had already left to go stay at his girlfriend's house.

It was Kaderli's idea that we should all bleed on a piece of wood that he had carved runes and white supremacy symbols into. I remember cursing myself for not bringing my own knife and having to use one of Lane's, which I prayed was clean. The knife had a broken tip, and I had no intention of slicing up my arm, so I furiously jabbed at my finger, managing to squeeze out just enough blood to take part.

We dripped our blood offering onto the carved piece of lumber and prayed to our gods. I don't know who Kaderli was praying to, but whatever was coming out of his mouth sounded demonic and gave me flashbacks to my wayward teenager days, when I had strayed from Christ. He later mentioned that he had a connection to some members of the

Order of Nine Angles (ONA or O9A), which was a UK-based Satanic occult group that promoted Nazism. I prayed alongside Lane and Andersson to gods of the Norse Pantheon—such as Thor, Odin, Ragnar. Kaderli prayed to gods of the Egyptian Pantheon.

The funny thing about Andersson was that I suspected *him* of being a confidential source during that weekend of training. He was asking direct questions as a cop would, like *who was Roman Wolf, why did he form The Base, where does he live, how was the group organized*—questions I was hoping to get answered, too, but didn't ask out of fear of being called out as a fed. But not long after that meetup, Andersson moved to the Ozarks and eventually left the group. He said he used to be with the U.S. Army National Guard but got kicked out due to his affiliation with white supremacy groups. I sent him a DM after he left the group and he said he had a job opportunity he couldn't pass up. "And the going plan now is getting a house with a lot of woods and seclusion," he wrote back. "I want to make my property a safehouse for our boys should they need a place to hang their hat outside of prying eyes."

Aside from prepping at the training camps, these meetups were also about creating propaganda. We would pose for photos in the woods—armed, dressed in Flecktarn camo, chosen by The Base because it's what Germans wore, and wearing the balaclavas to conceal our identities. We were very careful that nothing identifiable—tattoos, eyes, hair—was showing.

One of these photos of the four of us was posted to our Wire group.

"Good work as usual," Nazzaro wrote to me about the photo. "You've proven to be a valuable addition to our ranks . . . Keep it up."

I replied: "Honored!"

I rolled my truck up to Lane's property, ready to camp for yet another cell meeting. While I was still out of sight, I made sure to start my recordings.

I parked my truck and looked at the other cars in the driveway. *Okay, that's Helter Skelter's, that's Pestilence's . . . that's TMB's dad's car.* Then I looked down to the group that was sitting under the awning of the barn and counted the men. There seemed to be an extra person. I didn't have my glasses on—what a great part of aging—so couldn't be sure until I had walked down and was right in front of the stranger. He looked to be in his mid to late-twenties; reddish, messy hair; a huge, bushy beard. Then I heard him speak, and right away I thought, *That's a Canadian accent.* I had been a huge fan of *Strange Brew*, the 1983 movie with SCTV characters Bob and Doug McKenzie, played by comedians Dave Thomas and Rick Moranis. Bob and Doug lived on a diet of beer, back bacon, and donuts, and leaned into the stereotypical Canadian accent, ending most sentences with "eh."

"You probably know who I am," he said.

"Maybe?" I replied.

"I may or may not be from Canada," he said, then went on to tell me his moniker was Punished Snake.

And then it all clicked. Dave Arctorum, who then switched to Jimmy the Frog Rancher, who was actually the Canadian Army reservist Patrik Mathews, was now Punished Snake. He was renting a horse stall from Luke Lane's dad to sleep in. We'd found him!

Well, I'll be damned, I thought as I gave him a hug.

"Welcome to the United States, brother!"

14

THE WILD HUNT

Silver Creek, Georgia
October 31, 2019

I was exhausted. It had been a long day of training at the "hate camp" on Luke Lane's hundred-acre farm. There had been hand-to-hand combat, grappling, and weapon manipulation, along with pistol and rifle drills. It was survival training in anticipation of the Boogaloo—that day which The Base members believed society would collapse, a race war would ensue, and they would create their white ethnostate. Base cells were already looking at land in the Pacific Northwest, the Upper Peninsula of Michigan, and the Appalachian Mountains. One cell stated that they had recruited a nurse and a former chief of police, which they said would help build the infrastructure once the ethnostates were established.

A wicked cold front had swept through Georgia, with the temperature dropping approximately forty degrees in only a few hours. It hadn't been that cold all year, and it was a tough blow when you weren't acclimated. While the other guys were fumbling to set up their tents, I quietly retreated to my Ford 4x4 pickup truck for a rare moment alone and a chance to charge my phone. I just had to hope all my technology was working and everything was being recorded and transmitted.

My body ached from the cold. I was feeling every one of my nearly five decades on this earth. The cold was that type that settles deep in your bones and makes you extra weary. It was just four months into the case at this point and the pace had been nonstop. I had learned my lessons from Operation Roadkill and my subsequent "DNR," to know when to take a break, and I knew I'd eventually have to do that. But not tonight. Not yet. I blasted the heat in my truck and dozed off.

I woke to pounding on my window, not knowing if I had nodded off for mere minutes or hours. Someone was yelling, but I couldn't make out what they were saying.

I opened my eyes to see ZoomNat, a new member I had only met earlier that day. He was sporting a fresh bowl haircut in homage to mass murderer Dylann Roof. He said he had driven to Georgia to attend the camp from Austin, Texas, without stopping—more than nine hundred miles fueled on Adderall and Red Bull.

ZoomNat was with Kaderli, and as I rolled down the window Kaderli said, "Dude, you know about that ritual tonight?"

"Yeah."

"You know we're sacrificing a goat?" Kaderli asked.

"Yep," I replied unhappily.

"We just got the goat!"

I turned off my truck and opened the door to the frigid air, which quickly snapped me awake. I followed Kaderli through the pitch-black darkness until we reached Lemley's truck, where everyone was standing. Lemley looked at me and said this was "the Siege Goat." There, in the back, shaking, terrified, and shitting all over everything, was a goat they had stolen from a nearby property. One of the guys complained that the goat was shitting everywhere, and I said, "Well, I would be too if a bunch of guys wearing camouflage and masks and holding guns just took me out of my backyard and threw me in a truck!"

I looked down at the poor animal and tried to think of a way to stop what was about to happen, but a wave of dread spread through my body.

On our Wire group, various members had talked about an animal sacrifice and how this would signify the start of the "Wild Hunt." In pre-Christian Nordic mythology, the Wild Hunt was when the god Odin and his army went on a chaotic rampage in the fiercely cold and dark midwinter. Anyone who saw the ghostly procession would be carried away and dropped elsewhere, or worse.[1]

In The Base's twisted version of this ritual, the "Wild Hunt" would mark the start of their mission to "clean up" non-whites and Jews.

I noticed Bilbrough, a.k.a. Eisen, was petting the goat and speaking softly as he stood by Lemley's truck. "Eisen, is it bad that I feel sorry for the goat?" I asked him, hoping maybe he would take pity on the poor animal. He replied, "I mean, kind of."

Then he seemed to momentarily be lost in thought and added, "He will know where he's going before he dies. I'll try to make sure of that." Some other members were looking remorseful, and Bilbrough said, "Let's not even talk about this." He was determined to keep the mood positive because in his mind, the goat was about to make a beautiful sacrifice. He had named the goat "Gar," after his great-great-grandfather Garfield (which was also his middle name).

"I'm with ya. I'll just push that beach ball down in the water," I said as I watched the others making a harness to lead the goat to the ceremony; to lead Gar to his death.

I slipped away and went back to my truck. I looked around carefully, making sure I was in the clear, and leaned into my transmitting device to talk to my team. "So . . . I'm pretty sure we're getting ready to kill this goat. I can't think of a reason to stop it. If you guys don't want this to happen, let me know."

The team had set up their own camp in a nearby building. It was a twenty-four-hour operation as agents rotated through in shifts. If I was in the field—a team would be there to cover.

I waited a bit, hoping for a response. Nothing. "Okay. I guess we're doing this."

I rejoined the group and followed them deep into the woods.

—

It was Halloween night, and more members than usual had traveled to Georgia to attend this hate camp. There were approximately a dozen guys, who had come from all over the U.S.—Texas, Alabama, Michigan, Delaware. In addition to ZoomNat, there was Big Siege (he *was* big, about 350 pounds), Dema, and Apocryphon. They joined the members of our Georgia cell: TMB (Lane), Pestilence (Kaderli), and Helter Skelter / Skelter Helter (Helterbrand). And the Maryland cell was there, too: Cantgoback (Lemley, the Iraqi vet) and Eisen (Bilbrough).

The Canadian fugitive, Patrik Mathews, had been living at the farm since Lemley brought him here. I later learned that there was a Base member going by the online name Viking21 who had first picked him up after he fled Manitoba and dumped his red pickup truck near the border. Then Lemley and Bilbrough drove nearly six hundred miles from Maryland to southern Michigan to take Mathews back east. After dropping off Bilbrough in Maryland, Lemley continued south to Chincoteague, Virginia. That's when he posted on our group chat, "The objective has been reached," and PunishedSnake1488 was added to our group—a post I didn't understand at the time. By mid-September, Lemley had driven down to Georgia to bring Mathews to Lane's farm, and that's where I met him, and alerted our case teams that the Canadian had been located.[2]

I had spent hours and hours during my late September and early October trips to Georgia hiking with Mathews, or talking late in the night with him, along with Lane and Kaderli and sometimes others, recording everything they said. Mathews spoke emotionally at one point about an ex-fiancée he had been with for a year and a half. She was half-Black, and he said he would be forced to kill her when Western society collapsed, and National Socialists took over.

During one conversation, they all talked about their parents. Kaderli said he hoped once the West had collapsed, his parents would accept that National Socialism was the way to go. But Mathews said he already knew his dad did not accept that. "Any engagement in anti-fascist activity will carry the death penalty," he said. "I may very well be shooting him in the back of his fucking head. I'm not looking forward to that, but I accept that responsibility."

Kaderli paused and shook his head. He said, "You're further along than me. I couldn't execute my parents."

Then it was Lane's turn to respond. "I could kill my dad. I could," Lane said. "But I know for a fact . . . I know for a fact I'd be crying myself every day for the rest of my life." Then he paused, thought about that for a minute, and added, "I'd ask somebody else to do it."

Mathews was definitely the biggest talker in the group, and often sounded like he had nothing to lose, since he had already lost everything after being outed in Canada. He considered himself now a "ghost," and therefore gun and immigration laws didn't apply to him anymore, he said. "I only exist for the white revolution now," he told me.

Mathews also discussed creating a safehouse for other doxed members like him. He would form a team of ghosts to start retaliating against Antifa types. Mathews said he could easily look like a homeless person on the street and track his targets. Then when the time was right, he would shoot them in the back of the head with a revolver (which doesn't discharge brass, he noted).

His intentions and hatred were clear, but he was so talkative, I could already tell that he was starting to annoy some of the other members of the Georgia cell.

—

We all walked Gar-the-goat down to what Lane referred to as the "Holy Spot," and knelt in a circle. Most of the men had been drinking, and Bilbrough was holding a bladed object that looked like a machete as the goat trembled in the middle of our circle.

I remember I told Kaderli, "You assist him, and I'll hold the goat." Then Bilbrough gave a speech about the Wild Hunt and seemed nervous. He told us, "I'm gonna need everyone to pray over the goat. It needs to know where it's going. And it's going to the Elves and Odin." Bilbrough explained how the sacrifice would allow us to become part of the Wild Hunt, but he was breathing hard and kept saying, "You guys ready?" He did a couple practice swings in the air before striking the animal and said, "It might take two swings."

As I was holding the back of the goat all I could think was *Just get it over with.*

Someone in the group said out loud, "Just do it!"

Bilbrough reared the blade back, high over his head, and with all his energy brought it down on the goat's neck. *THUNK.*

The goat barely flinched. I'm not sure if even a hair was cut on his neck. Obviously, Bilbrough had no idea how thick the backstrap of a goat was. As I continued to hold the back end of the goat, the others began yelling, "Strike again."

"Harder!"

"We might need a saw."

"It's the hair!"

I thought, *Oh, this is going to get ugly.*

Kaderli stepped in and asked if anyone had a gun. No one was supposed to, as that had been one of the conditions before we came down here, to check our firearms. But then ZoomNat stepped forward. Perfect, the one who hadn't slept in at least forty-eight hours, and who was the most uncoordinated and inexperienced with weapons, apparently didn't get the memo.

Lane took the gun from ZoomNat and gave it to Bilbrough, who was now fueled by adrenaline and the embarrassment of the failed sacrifice attempt. He pointed the gun toward Gar as if he was going to shoot . . . but then looked away!

Everyone was circled around the goat and some of us were holding it. The firearms / tactical instructor in me kicked in. I yelled out, "Hey. Hey! Watch when you do it! Don't look away because you're going to miss if you do."

Bilbrough moved closer and placed the gun next to the goat's temple. *Boom!* The sound of the shot echoed through the woods and Gar went down.

But as he lay there, his legs were still kicking. I'm not sure how long he twitched like that, but it felt like forever. A debate ensued about whether the animal was still alive, or if it was just postmortem reflexes. Finally, I convinced Bilbrough to take another shot. *Boom!* One member said, "Yeah, he's definitely dead now." Another said it was all okay because "he knows where he's going." If only the goat could have told us if that was what he really thought.

Its throat was slashed, and a cup was filled with his blood.

Oh, but the night wasn't over yet. Bilbrough pulled out a sheet of acid. He told the others that taking a tab would help them along their shamanic journey and make it easier for them to enter the spirit world. One by one he approached the members, who waited on their knees in a circle. They would put the hit of acid on, or just under, their tongue, and drink the goat's blood, as if taking communion on Sunday.

I followed Bilbrough, using my flashlight to guide his way. I knew that for many of them, this would be their first time ever "tripping." *Angry white supremacists with a lot of guns and ammo on acid? What could possibly go wrong?*

When it came to Lane, he took the acid and *then* started asking a rapid-fire volley of questions about what it would do to him. *Little late.* Only a few members chose not to partake in the acid, and that, of course, included me.

It didn't take long for the goat's blood to coagulate into a thick red goop with big chunks as the members choked it down. There was no way I was going to drink that, so when it was handed to me, I put my finger in the red sludge and brought it to my mouth and sucked the blood off my finger, then passed it along.

Apparently, the big chunks were too much for Big Siege. He stepped away from the circle and started vomiting.

Happy f'in Halloween.

The next day was completely shot. Everyone was either too hungover, or still tripping with their hallucinations that kept them up all night. I wasn't the only one who didn't take the acid, so luckily it didn't look suspicious.

I went for a morning breakfast run to get us some food, and a moment of peace to not be Pale Horse. I came back loaded down with savory Bojangles bacon, egg, and cheese biscuits, which had been smelling delicious the whole drive back to the farm. "Pale Horse!" said Mathews. "You've gotta try this goat." The goat had been skinned during the night with my personal knife (which I remembered this time), and we had thrown its innards into the creek. While I was gone, Mathews had been trying to cook the meat over a fire. It was the most gamey meat I had ever tasted. Let's just say after one bite I secretly gave the rest to one of the dogs. Then I ate a biscuit as fast as I could to get that taste out of my mouth.

By day three, we were doing pseudo-military training again: target practice, armed patrolling techniques, and firearm drills. Everything was being filmed because the propaganda—the recruiting video we were about to produce—was just as important as the training itself. The Base wanted every new recruitment video to be better than the last. During the training we carried the goat's head everywhere with us, posing with it for photos, dressed in our finest attire of Flecktarn camo and with The Base flag behind us.

At one point mid-afternoon, Lane told us we would soon break for lunch, but asked us to put away our weapons first and meet him behind the barn. I could see that he and Mathews were exchanging looks. Something didn't feel right.

When we arrived behind the barn, Lane, who was holding a revolver in his hand, instructed us to put our phones in airplane mode, place them in a container, and form a line. Mathews was holding Lane's rifle and Helterbrand had that Geiger counter wand device that had almost led to my demise on my first meeting with them when they scanned my truck.

But this wasn't like the basement search by the Outlaws on the Operation Roadkill case. Or like that first vetting meeting with Lane and Kaderli. There were no transmitting devices on my body, so as soon as Lane told us to form a line, I stepped up first. When I passed, Helterbrand said, "I knew I didn't have to worry about you."

One by one, he moved down the line, wanding all the members as everyone shifted uncomfortably. There was nervous laughter, and someone asked, "What if we take off?" Mathews replied, "You'll get shot. I gotta do what I gotta do." More nervous laughter.

I may have looked cool and calm, but I was closely paying attention to the other members. I didn't know several of their true identities. What if there was an Antifa member or journalist? It wouldn't be the first time. What would I do if the detection device found something? More importantly, what would Lane and Mathews do?

But the wand didn't make a sound.

And exhale.

The day would end with another hate camp ritual as we went back to our ceremony spot in the woods. Lane would film the whole thing so it could be used in The Base's recruitment video, but this time it was the American flag and Bibles we'd be burning, not an animal sacrifice.

ZoomNat went to burn the American flag first, and as he was trying to put the flag in the fire, he almost fell in. A huge part of me wanted to just let that play out, but I grabbed the other side of the flag. Members chanted "Fuck America!" as it burned.

Then, it was time for the Bibles. The Bibles were placed open, face down in the flames. "Fuck your Jewish God!" "Fuck Jesus!" they yelled as the blaze flickered. Mathews seemed fascinated with the fire as it started to die down, and kept stoking the coals. While he was doing so, a Bible flipped open. To everyone's surprise, we saw that not a single page had been burned. Mathews began tearing pages out one by one. Again, the fire blazed up, and eventually it began dying down. Just as before, Mathews began to stoke the coals to keep the fire going. Do you want to guess what happened next? Yep. A second Bible flipped open to reveal no pages were burned. At this point, Big Siege loudly proclaimed, "Man, these Bibles just won't fucking burn!"

Internally, I pictured myself high-fiving God.

I know there are scientific reasons you could cite why the Bibles wouldn't burn—how the pages are packed tightly, or maybe they're made with nonflammable paper. You can think what you want, but I know what I believe. This was a sign that I was not alone. Later that night, when I was back in my hotel looking at photos from the day, I enlarged the photo of the fire and could clearly read "Holy Bible" amid the flames.

The new Base recruiting video was posted to their various channels that winter. To a soundtrack of pounding rock music, you could see us moving through the woods wearing masks and camouflage, automatic weapons at the ready. Cut to combat training and then a group of us emptying our automatic weapons in a terrifying display of gunfire, which is referred to as a magazine dump. The video ends with us marching with torches through the dark to set fire to the Bibles and an American flag.

The whole video was only a minute long but would be effective in attracting more recruits from around the world.

I remember driving home after that long, long weekend feeling tired and shell-shocked. When I got up the next day, I texted my pastor. Much like someone taking a long shower after they've been covered in filth, I needed to be prayed over.

15
THE CAMPING TRIP

Knoxville, Tennessee
December 3, 2019

I had prepared my family ahead of time. I was about to go on a Pale Horse call, so no loud noises, no talking. I walked into a spare room by the kitchen, which I liked to call our "bonus room," and locked the door. I began the recording, noting the date and time. Then I pulled up the encrypted app Wire on my phone and heard its distinctive chimes as I hoped TMB would answer.

"How you doin', brother!" I said when I heard Lane pick up.

I hadn't been back to Georgia since the Halloween hate camp. A couple days before I made that call, Lane had sent a list of what we needed for our next cell meetup at his farm, which was scheduled for December 13–14. He called it a "fun family-friendly camping trip."

The packing list included such items as a nondescript hoodie without any logos, brand names, or designs, which he advised us to buy from a thrift store and pay cash. None of the clothes we brought should be identifiable as something we would normally wear, he wrote, and if we had leather gloves or latex gloves, bring 'em.

Lane was always good with his OPSEC. He had sent impressive instructions like this to our Wire chat previously about how to go "postering" without being detected. Postering, flyering, or stickering was what the Base members called their mission to put up propaganda flyers with contact information, to attract recruits. They even had posters with QR codes that would take people to our recruitment material, including the Halloween propaganda video.

In addition to Lane's OPSEC guide, he had also sent me other readings to prepare for the Boogaloo. They included step-by-step guides on how to build a 9mm bullet hose submachine gun, or homemade C-4, and there were instructions on land navigation or how to spot law enforcement. Many of the readings were older U.S. Army or Marines field manuals, but there were some original Base materials, too, like the ten-page "Fieldcraft Basic Training Guide." It began, "There is a fine line between order and chaos and sometimes that line can be measured in seconds. When every second counts, having a plan and the tools to see that plan through are crucial to survival. A 72-Hour Emergency Kit packed with survival essentials is a priceless resource in any Bug Out scenario."

When I first got the text, I thought maybe the upcoming December trip was just about postering around Rome, Georgia, and Lane wanted us to be extra cautious. But then Kaderli, who had started to call himself "Hound" in our chat group instead of "Pestilence," asked if he should bring a gun.

Lane wrote back, "Bring the sub." (Which referred to Kaderli's KelTec SUB2000 9mm semiautomatic rifle.)

When I further inquired about whether I needed to bring "all my guns/gear? Ammo?" Lane wrote back, "Yes."

None of this sounded good. The pressure was on from the Atlanta FBI team to try to find out what was being planned so we could stop it if we had to. This call was my attempt to get Lane to tell me *anything* more about a planned meetup.

"I guess it's supersecret. I'm just trying to figure out what to pack, what to bring," I said.

But Lane was being frustratingly aloof, and every so often would just let out a little giggle.

"I don't have a damn sleeping bag. I'm going to sleep in my damn truck," I said, and he replied cryptically, "If you sleep at all."

When I mentioned how surprised I was about all the items that he wanted us to bring, he started laughing again, so I just chuckled along with him. The call was going nowhere.

But I tried again. "I'm like, do I have to bring a fucking different vehicle?"

He answered, "If you want, because I don't know whose car we're riding in. Probably be either yours or Helter's." I was hoping he would say that my truck was fine (low-risk operation) or that I should find a vehicle that couldn't be traced back to me (high-risk operation). But he refused to divulge any more.

"I'm just trying to figure it out, because I'm an old man and like to know what the fuck I'm going to be doing." *Awkward silence.*

By the time the call ended, I still didn't know what I was supposed to be doing.

—

On December 5, two days later, I tried another call. This time it was the evening, and I sipped a little Crown Royal, making small talk as the ice tinkled in my glass, about how I was tired of Jack Daniel's. Lane sounded bored and eager to get off the phone.

I pretended the main purpose of the call was getting his help to vet a potential new member from Indiana, who Nazzaro had asked me to meet in person. Lane said it wouldn't be a problem to help, and our vetting trip wouldn't delay his December 13 plans. It gave me another opening to subtly ask about those plans.

"Here's my thing. If I'm bringing weapons, are the weapons going to be in my car when we're going to do what we're doing?"

"Yours will be inside," he replied.

"It'll be what? Inside the car?"

"Inside your car."

Once again, his answers were short (and short on details).

"I'm not saying I don't trust you," I said. "I'm saying I'm not where I'm at because I've done stupid shit. I've *seen* stupid shit . . . but I'm here without a record for a reason."

Finally, I got to him. He agreed to tell me more, but not on our Wire call; he said we would have to do it in person. "Ah fuck, maybe I'll swing . . . What is today? Thursday? God dang it," I said, although I knew of course I would get there as soon as possible. "I could swing through . . . maybe tomorrow or Saturday?"

As soon as I was off the call, I alerted the Atlanta case team. They were ready to roll, and we did.

The next day I stood outside Lane's barn, pounding on the door. It was early afternoon on December 6, cold and raining as it always seemed to be in the fall and winter months I visited. I was getting no response. I tried texting instead as I grew impatient. "Wake your ass up," I wrote.

After I'd been sitting there for about thirty-five minutes, worrying the trip was a bust, finally Lane came down. "Morning, sunshine!" I greeted him.

We both knew why I was there. So we put our phones on airplane mode and placed them in a cooler and then walked over to the edge of the barn and got right down to business. I said, "Now, you know I'm a jokester, and I like to joke. But when it's time to be serious, I can be serious. So, what?"

Lane was still grinning.

"Essentially," he said, "we're going to whack some people."

—

Murder was a hot topic of conversation among Base members. Our chats were full of people vowing to knock off journalists or Antifa activists, or essentially anyone who wasn't white. But no matter how chilling it all sounded, the intent to kill an unspecified target in the name of bringing on the Boogaloo wasn't a criminal offense. Even Mathews's comments about having to kill his dad when Western society collapsed weren't enough, without a specific action that showed he was preparing and ready to carry out the deed, something in legal terms we'd call "acts in furtherance of" a crime.

We just had many vague, recorded conversations like this:

"These Antifa types, all these people. There has to start being consequences for what they are and that's race traitors and agents of the system," Mathews said at one point. "You know, if you really want to fight these evil, evil Nazis you better be prepared for when they actually start becoming what you—"

Kaderli interrupted, "What you've vilified them to be."

"Yeah," said Mathews.

"You call them neo-Nazis enough, they'll eventually show you what a neo-Nazi terrorist is," said Kaderli.

Mathews replied, "Makes me wonder if they're ever really prepared for that day to come?"

"Absolutely not," Lane chimed in.

Kaderli later complained, "I wanna fuckin' fight something, dude. I'm so tired."

Lane promised, "We'll get the body dropping shit done."[1]

There had been just one previous breakthrough in our conversations. Something a little more specific. It was on the last day of the Halloween hate camp, when it was just me, Lane, and Kaderli who were left. We sat around the fire talking well into the early morning hours. I casually brought up a past conversation that they had had with Mathews earlier in the month. I noted that they had all lowered their voices, seemingly trying to hide something, so I politely asked now what they had been talking about. Lane bent over to Kaderli and whispered something I couldn't hear. Then Kaderli said, "Yeah, I think we can trust him."

Before he went on, like usual, Lane requested that our phones be put in airplane mode. Then they told me there were some lefty Antifa types they had identified, and they were working on a plan to retaliate against these people for their affiliations. It was a significant conversation, and I remember alerting the case team as soon as I could. This is where you want to be as an undercover—I had finally gained their full trust. They wanted to include me in activities we had not been privy to.

But *what?!* We still didn't have a specific plan.

Now we did.

Our hunch that something was brewing for the December 13 meetup was right. Lane had worked out a plan and had picked a date to "whack" the Antifa activists.

I settled in to hear more, with two goals in mind: get as many details as possible about his plan, and slow him down to buy us time.

The murders were to take place in seven days.

—

As we sat under the awning of the barn, Lane told me the names and addresses of the people he intended to murder. They were a man and woman from nearby Bartow County, Georgia, and according to Lane, they were a "high-ranking Antifa couple." He later corrected himself, saying Antifa didn't really have ranks, but this couple was very active with the group Atlanta Antifascists. Lane said it was Kaderli who had found the names of the targets, and he would participate in the killings along with Helterbrand. If I was willing, they wanted me on board, too.

Lane had originally planned to include Mathews, but he now believed he was incompetent. Mathews had definitely overstayed his welcome in Georgia. After the Halloween weekend, Lemley took him back to Maryland to be a part of that cell, and soon after the relations between the two groups soured.

As I was processing everything Lane was telling me, my mind was racing to try to come up with ways to slow him down, but not look like I had cold feet. I pointed out to him that he had done very little prep. I compared it to how thorough he was in the planning of postering, and that was night and day compared to this. I mean, we're talking about killing people, I told him!

Then it hit me: I'm a site survey specialist! This is what I do when looking at properties to buy. *Is it mercantile, is it residential, what are the demographics of the area, crime, schools, ethnicity?* Since Lane had so little information of the actual address and was worried about being connected to the crime by searching on the web or driving by, I convinced him that I could get it and it would look legit because I would be looking at adjacent areas while pulling the couple's info. I asked him why he was being so hasty on this. He replied that he was just tired of waiting to do something.

But Lane listened to me carefully. He was impatient, but he wasn't dumb and had no desire to martyr himself with this murder. He agreed to let me do my research, which would help delay the killings.

At the end of our talk, he tore me off a piece of paper to write on, saying that was safer than giving me the whole pad, because it could leave indentations. Then he showed me details on his phone, and I wrote down what I needed, including the couple's names.

—

I drove back to Georgia on December 13, the day we were supposed to murder an Antifa couple, had I not slowed down their plot. It was rainy and cold, once again, and I eased my truck up the long dirt road to the barn. Lane's dad, Tom, and the dogs came out to greet me first. Kaderli came out next.

One of the key virtues for being an undercover agent, as I've said often, is patience, and the Base case sure required a lot of it. Before Lane joined us, I engaged in at least an hour of small talk with Kaderli—the traffic, the weather, weight lifting and testosterone shots. Finally, I eased us back to Base gossip. In addition to the *Vice* article, there had been recent news about a Michigan cell member, who went by the name AK. He had gone to the home of a local Antifa podcaster and taken photos of himself wearing our trademark skull balaclava and dressed in camo and a bulletproof vest. "That'll make someone scared!" Kaderli said excitedly. (AK was actually twenty-five-year-old Base member Justin Watkins, who would be arrested about a year later.[2])

Finally, Lane and Thomas Andersson joined us. Andersson was back in town for the month, but it would be the last time I'd see him. I knew that he wasn't involved in the plot, so we were going to have to discuss the trip privately, which meant that for another four or five hours, we sat around, just talking about everything and nothing.

Now, don't get me wrong, I'm a talker. But sitting all day, in the icy rain, with guys who are about twenty years my junior and have such a warped view on the world, well, let's just say it's tiring.

By the end of the day, as I was getting ready to head to my hotel for the night, I took Lane aside and we lowered our voices. He told me Helterbrand—who wasn't with us on this trip—was definitely in on the plan. He didn't know any of the details yet, but Lane had no doubt about his intentions.

He's "big into Bowl Patrol stuff, you know, Dylann Roof," he said to me about the mass murderer with a bowl haircut. Lane said Helterbrand had asked him before: "When are we going to church?"

The next day I returned so we could do some reconnaissance on the house of the Antifa couple. I had put Florida plates on my truck, telling Lane and Kaderli I just had taken them off a car while traveling for a job and wanted to be safe in case anyone saw us today.

Lane had come a long way from where we were a week ago and planned the operation in precise detail. This was what he had in mind: I would drive the two of them, along with Helterbrand, and drop them off. Lane and Kaderli would try to use a lock-pick gun to get in, and if that wasn't quick enough, Lane would just use a sledgehammer. Helterbrand would have an AR-style rifle and stand guard on the front porch, as Lane and Kaderli would get inside and kill the victims, preferably with revolvers. Lane explained that they preferred revolvers because of the fact that they didn't leave shell casings, although he did ask me to buy "brass bags," just in case. (A brass bag attaches to your rifle to catch all the ejected brass.) And he told me to buy them out of state and from different stores. Don't get all four bags in one spot, he said, and if anyone asked me why I needed them, I was instructed to say that I wanted them for reloading purposes.

He planned that first we would set up a camping spot in the woods. Our phones and any electronics would stay there. Then we would go to a cheap motel room that he had rented, and we would all take showers. That way, we could rub off any dead skin, eliminating the risk of any of it flaking off and leaving our DNA while we were committing the crime. We would wear long leather gloves that we could tuck into our shirtsleeves and then tape to the sleeves. He reiterated his instructions not to wear Base clothing, or anything identifiable. Wear boots instead of sneakers,

Lane said, so our pants could be tucked in and also taped, once again to avoid dead skin falling off. We would put Vaseline on our eyebrows and eyelashes.

Once the murders were done, we would burn the house down and return to the campsite. It was a pretty decent plan (if you didn't have an undercover agent as part of your crew).

Helterbrand wasn't there for that meeting, so we arranged to come back a week later to get him the details. Anything we would discuss online we would use a cypher code—a combination of numbers and letters—that Lane had devised for us. "37C" would be the code for the murders, also known as the "camping trip." "32W" meant "planning the murder" and "59B" meant we should meet at Lane's farm.

—

The pace was relentless and a little bit frantic by the end of 2019. When not doing undercover work, I would often be on back-to-back Skype calls with divisions around the U.S. and headquarters on this case. I remember one of my friends, who was an analyst, looked over at me at one point and said, "I'm exhausted just watching you work." And I was still a case agent, the undercover coordinator, and the lead tactical / defensive tactics instructor for our division. Does this sound familiar? Was I headed down the same path of destruction from my Outlaws case? No. I had learned my lesson at the end of Operation Roadkill. This time, my life was more balanced with family and church, and I was better at handling stress. I'm not saying it was easy, especially as I was aging, but I knew how to relax and recharge.

I remember one evening sitting out on the back porch with Kara, having some adult beverages, and telling her about all the stuff I had been doing. She mentioned that she was always praying over me when I was gone, and for some reason her comment caught me a little off guard and I giggled. I said something like, "We've been doing this a long time together. You don't need to worry about me."

Kara got very serious and looked me directly in the eyes. She said, "I'm your wife, and it is my job to cover you." Cover me in prayers. Her sincerity was so moving, I apologized for taking her comments lightly, and thanked her for always being there for me.

As I drove back to Lane's farm on December 19, I knew I had not only my case team covering me, but Kara, too.

Helterbrand was at the farm this time, and there was little doubt he was incredibly enthusiastic about the planned murders. He had a few OPSEC questions about whether the couple had a security system, and noted how loud pistols could be, offering to bring "solvent traps" to act as a silencer.

Then he asked if the couple had children.

Lane confessed that he didn't know, but added that if there were, they would "probably just leave them."

"I mean," Helterbrand responded, "I've got no problem killing a commie kid."

He later offered to steal some license plates, and bring Adderall "to help keep people up," or he would "smoke some meth and go clear the house."

Lane laughed. "That's race-war-ready!"

"This is what I've been fantasizing about for about two years now," Helterbrand replied.[3]

There was just one issue. An OPSEC problem they had identified. Two Base members—Canadian fugitive Patrik Mathews (Punished Snake) and Iraqi war vet Brian Lemley (Cantgoback) knew about their murder plan.

But that's okay, Lane assured me. Because we were going to kill them, too.

16

THE BOOGALOO

Newark, Delaware
January 11, 2020

"Chaos would be great," Brian Lemley said to his roommate Patrik Mathews. After an afternoon of shooting, they were enjoying a couple drinks and talking excitedly about their plans. "Like, I'm hoping that one of these guys is acting like a fucking looney tune and some cop takes him down, to try to like disarm him, and his buddies just open fire. And . . . so once that happens you would have like a hasty retreat and like kind of like . . . a running skirmish out of the city—"

Mathews interrupted. "It would be an escalation of violence. It would be like the initial violence would cause some military police . . . it would be basically what's called the three block war, which was where there was a situation in Iraq where there was four or five different combatant groups and about a three block area and they were all fighting against each other and there were American troops on the ground where corporals had to make decisions on the ground and leadership because they could not, the the"—he couldn't get the words out fast enough—"the situation was so complex that they had to act on their own because it was changing that fast. That's what's probably going to fucking happen . . . Basically, in a nutshell, it's going to be a complete and total fucking shit show the minute violence kicks off."[1]

Lemley and Mathews were formerly military men, but they weren't talking about some far-off war. They were planning this mayhem right here at home, in Virginia.

I was lying on the floor of their filthy apartment, stretching my back, carefully listening, and throwing out questions or comments every so often to keep them talking. My back was killing me. The pain had been so bad the previous week with spasms, we had to postpone my trip there. The only way I was able to manage the flight from Tennessee to Maryland the night before was thanks to TENS (transcutaneous electrical nerve stimulation), which is essentially a unit with pads that send jolts of electricity to reduce the pain. What I would find out several months later, after an MRI and CT scan, was that my original lumbar fusion had broken, and I would need surgery. For now, I was just running that TENS 24-7 with the exception of showering, because with the Base case, time was of the essence.

This was my first in-person visit with Mathews or Lemley since they left the Halloween hate camp in Georgia, although we stayed in touch by texting in our Wire group, and sometimes I called them. They had rented a one-bedroom apartment and moved in together in Delaware. Their relationship with the other members of the Georgia cell may have gone south, but they were still talking to me.

I remember one call in early December where we talked about our fears of an informant, which had been a hot topic among Base members. There had been another *Vice* article reporting on the Halloween hate camp. Mathews, as usual, was talking *at* me, more than *with* me, imparting his knowledge about infiltrators. "Feds will not do drugs. It's an old telltale thing. If you want to fucking see if someone's a fucking snitch or something, I dunno if you're dealing dope or something, if you offer them some dope and they don't smoke it. That's a good chance they're a fucking fed," he said, having no idea how ironic his comments were.

He was also giving us his hard-earned advice about how not to be doxed if we were vetting new members. He knew he had made bad OPSEC choices in meeting Canadian journalist Ryan Thorpe. Give a fake name, he said, plus a false job description and hometown. He cautioned us not to park where they can see you, so they can't ID your car, and make sure you're the one asking all the questions, not the other way around. "Prod their worldview," he said, adding that you should make sure they can use racial slurs naturally.

Even though I hadn't been in the same room with them throughout November and December, FBI Special Agent Rachid Harrison and his squad out of the Baltimore Division, along with Assistant United States Attorney Thomas Windom, were working around the clock monitoring the Delaware Base cell and building a case. One day in December, when their apartment was empty, an FBI "sneak and peek" team went in and installed recording devices in the walls (per what we call a "Title III wiretap") and executed a search warrant. Rachid would call me often to update me on what they were seeing and hearing. It was crazy, and alarming.

When Lemley and Bilbrough left Georgia, they brought Mathews back with them, along with 1,550 rounds of 5.56 ammunition that they had bought to add to their growing cache. That was enough ammunition to do some serious damage. They continued to build up their kit, ordering more rounds online, along with bulletproof vests and other tactical gear. Both Lemley and Mathews were managing to hold down jobs—Lemley was continuing to drive trucks and Mathews got a part-time construction gig that paid him cash and didn't check for a Social Security number. His crew was largely undocumented Hispanics who got along well with Mathews. Apparently he was good at hiding his true desires to kill anyone non-white.[2]

When agents executed the search warrant, they found a sniper rifle and what appeared to be components necessary to build an assault-style "ghost gun" along with survivalist gear and a stockpile of MREs (meals ready-to-eat).

They also found a self-recorded video Mathews had made where he was ranting in anti-Semitic and racist language. Mathews was wearing a gas mask, and as he spoke, he took long, deep breaths that sounded eerily like Darth Vader. His voice was slightly muffled, but his Canadian accent was still identifiable. "The time for words has ended. The time for podcasts has ended. The time for talk has ended. If you're wasting your time simply thinking there's going to be a movementarian approach to the coming problems, you think that podcasts are the solution, they're not, if you think talking is a solution, it is not. If you think politics is a solution, you are a damn fool," he begins.

"Option number one, prepare for the collapse. Option number two, bring the collapse. That is it. If you are not getting physically fit, if you are not getting armed, if you do not acquire weapons, ammunition, and training right fucking now, then you should be preparing to do what needs to be done. Derail some fucking trains, kill some people, and poison some water supplies. You better be fucking ready to do those things. If not, then you are not going to be ready for what's coming. If you want the white race to survive, you're going to have to do your fucking part."

On another recording he says, "They want bad guys so bad they can have it. We will give them white supremacist terrorists if that's what they want. Give them what they want. Give them what they deserve."

We had to find out—and find out fast—what we "deserved."

—

Brian Lemley Jr. was not a stranger to white nationalism. Back in November 2017, three months after the Charlottesville "Unite the Right" rally, he had reached out to the Northwest Front to get an "intro packet." Six days later, he contacted them again and asked to "have a conversation with an actual person that has the authority to discuss bloodlines."

The Northwest Front was created by Harold Covington, a longtime fringe figure in the neo-Nazi movement who wanted to create a white ethnostate in the Pacific Northwest. He envisioned a union of Washington State, Oregon, Idaho, and western Montana, which he said would be "kind of like the white version of Israel. I don't see why the Jews are the only people on Earth that get their own country and everyone else has to be diverse." Covington, who died in 2018 but left his legacy, had no objections to being called a racist. "Of course it's racism. What's wrong with racism? It's the purist form of patriotism," he once said.[3]

But Lemley didn't have much luck joining the group, despite repeated attempts. In one correspondence he confessed to having some Jewish heritage because he had to "get it off my chest." "Its come to my attention there is a jew in my family tree. My great grandmother on my mother's side was a pole with red hair and blue eyes last name greenberg. I decided to disclose this even though it may harm me. [*sic*]"[4] By 2018, he had managed to successfully join another white supremacy group, called the League of the South. He attended their Christmas party in Tennessee.

Then on February 27, 2019, when Lemley was thirty-two years old, he made his first contact with The Base, and was asked to fill out the same questionnaire I would get five months later. For military experience, he wrote that he had spent four years as a U.S. cavalry scout and had a fifteen-month tour in Iraq where he was a driver and radio operator and was in the Stryker Brigade. For "Science or Engineering training," he wrote, "just a trucker sorry." He also added, "Im a 2016 redpill. [*sic*]"

A "red pill" is a common expression in extremist movements and signifies the "awakening" to whatever particular belief—in his case, National Socialism. The expression goes back to the 1999 Hollywood movie *The Matrix*, where Keanu Reeves is offered a chance to see the world the way it really is by taking the red pill, or to take the blue pill and remain as he is, oblivious to the truth.[5]

Mathews, who had just turned twenty-seven when I met him, also had a military background, as a reservist combat engineer with the Canadian Armed Forces. His parents were divorced, but he was close with both of them and had a good upbringing, despite times when he was bullied as a kid. Mathews was also an animal lover (although that didn't seem to stop him from taking part in the Halloween ritual). Before he left Canada for the U.S., he made sure to find homes for his four cats.

—

This is what I knew, before meeting Lemley and Mathews that day:

On December 21, as agents in Baltimore were listening to the conversations in their apartment, they started talking about a "Virginia plan." The pair had posted about this plan on our Wire chat, too, but when they weren't getting everyone jumping on their bandwagon, they stopped writing about it. On that December day, though, unaware they were being recorded, they vowed to "fucking like shut down highways" or derail train lines. The idea was that they would generally "kick off the economic collapse of the U.S. within a week after the Boog starts." Boog, for Boogaloo.

They both believed the Boogaloo would begin on January 20, 2020, in Richmond, Virginia.[6] Since the November 2019 state elections, both chambers of the Virginia legislature and the governor's seat were controlled by the Democrats, who were proposing several gun control bills that would limit handgun purchases and require background checks, among other regulations. There was a pro-firearms rally scheduled for the twentieth on the grounds of the state capital in Richmond, Virginia, and tens of thousands were expected to attend—everyone from gun enthusiasts, to armed militias, to anti-government extremist groups like the Oath Keepers and the Proud Boys. Lemley and Mathews believed this would be their chance to create chaos, spark the Boogaloo, and accelerate society's collapse. It was their "Virginia plan."

Mathews was overheard saying, "Something that a lot of people don't know, a lot of race riots back in the day were started by whites. We would start the riots and you best believe we finished them. We need to bring that back. We need to go back to the days of fucking decimating Blacks and getting rid of them wherever they stand. If you see a bunch of Blacks sitting on some corner you fucking shoot them."

Their racism and misogyny as they spoke to each other was nonstop. "Make your community a non-welcome community. Some bitch decides to fuck a n*****. You fucking hang her," Mathews said. "Some fucking n****** come into your town and start selling drugs, hang 'em. Kill 'em. If you do nothing, that tells them they're welcome." Lemley referred to white women who were with Black men as "coal burners." "I'm literally gonna shove my gun into a coal burner's mouth, drive her up the wall, and blow her head off."

A couple days before Christmas their talk turned to murdering law enforcement officers to get additional gear that they needed for the Boogaloo. "Guy, is just like sitting there, he's just parked in his . . . in his car and sitting in his . . . in his driver's seat and not moving he's just sitting there," Lemley said. "And all I have to do is . . . is plink him right through the fucking windshield . . . and everything is now mine . . ." Although both men were military trained, they were not especially skilled snipers. They did have thermal scopes, though—Lemley's rifle had a particularly good one that cost him $6,000. This equipment would allow them to be night snipers, which they saw as a way to even the playing field against law enforcement once the Boogaloo began.

At one point, Mathews seemed to stop and think about all their talk and what it meant. He said to Lemley, "I'm worried we're going to become psychopaths. It's kind of scary if you think about it. I mean . . . like as to what we are slowly becoming?"

Lemley assured him, "I need to claim my first victim . . . You need to get that anxiety of the first one out of the way."

They also talked in grandiose terms about ridiculous plots like springing Dylann Roof from the heavily fortified maximum security federal prison USP Terre Haute. Mathews said at one point, "We should just go and just break out every fucking saint. Can you imagine? Can you imagine Dylann Roof broked out of jail? The Base would be known as the guys who broke out Dylann Roof." Accelerationist groups referred to mass murderers who were driven by racial hatred as "saints." They even had what they called a "Saint Leader Board," where they would rank murderers by their kills. "Saint Breivik" was Norwegian terrorist Anders Behring Breivik, who detonated a van bomb in Oslo, killing eight, then slaughtered sixty-nine participants in a Workers' Youth League summer camp on the island of Utoya in 2011. Many of his victims were teenagers. "Saint Tarrant" was twenty-eight-year-old Brenton Harrison Tarrant, who earlier that year went on a shooting rampage in two mosques in Christchurch, New Zealand, during prayer time, killing fifty-one and injuring forty others.

Also recorded was a conversation between Lemley and Mathews about assassinating the speaker of the Virginia House of Delegates, who had just been elected and was the first woman to lead the House in the state's four-hundred-year history.[7] They got her address from the Internet. In their twisted logic, they believed killing her could "accelerate their [the House's] gun control agenda," which would provoke a violent reaction and help their cause. After a little bit of research, they decided there wasn't a good sniper location near the speaker's residence, so they started to look into attacking her on her way to work.

Then, on January 7, a few days before I arrived, Lemley ordered another fifteen hundred rounds of 5.56 mm and 6.5 mm ammunition to fit the two firearms we knew they had.

—

The morning I arrived, I pulled into Newark and went on the search for a good coffee shop. I knew I'd need that caffeine jolt. With the Baltimore team covering me at a distance, I called Lemley as soon as I arrived at his apartment complex, and he came out with Mathews. We gave each other big, brotherly hugs.

I helped them load up Lemley's truck with all our weapons and gear and drove to a nearby public shooting range to help them zero in their new scopes. We were there for hours, and by the time we hit a drive-thru, we were all hungry and eagerly gulped down our burgers in the car. On the way back to their apartment, we stopped by Lemley's mother's house to pick up the ammunition he had ordered. He thought it was safer sending the shipment there, than to an apartment he shared with a fugitive. One more stop, to the liquor store, and we settled into their messy one-bedroom home.

As the evening wore on, they talked more and more, and I moved from the floor to sit at their kitchen table, Lemley on my left and Mathews on my right.

"We gotta pick up where Pierce and all the other ones failed. We gotta act when it's time to act. We can't fail where they have failed or else the white race is extinct," Mathews said, referring to William Pierce, who wrote *The Turner Diaries.*

Aside from *Siege*, this book was probably the most influential text among white supremacists. Written in 1978, the novel depicts an attack on the Capitol by white supremacists trying to overthrow the government. "The real value of all our attacks today lies in the psychological impact, not the immediate casualties," the 1978 novel's narrator, Earl

Turner, writes in his diary. "They learned this afternoon that not one of them is beyond our reach." (This reference and the book would later take on new relevance after the January 6 attack on the Capitol.)[8]

Mathews turned his talk to Virginia: "We shoot at the government. We kill the fucking cops. We blast the fucking Nat [National] Guard. What we do is we provide covering fire . . . and assistance . . ."

Lemley: "We're little green men essentially."

I cut in. "If they start engaging cops and everybody starts going, we start picking up from far away?"

Lemley: "We jump right in. We jump in . . . We wanna ambush. We don't want to . . . we don't want to like line fight?"

"But if it's only the three of us," I asked, "how do we ambush? We just . . ."

"We'll be doing night, night operations," Lemley replied.

"Okay," I said. "Who am I killing?"

Now it was Mathews's turn to explain. "I'll give you the meat and the bones. We don't have to reveal that we are National Socialists. We just have to reveal to these NS [National Socialist] guys err I mean to these patriots etcetera . . . that we are the good guys . . . we're on your side . . . and we fucking kill the fucking government which is the fucking enemy."

"Thereby we are helping the acceleration," I added.

"Well, yeah. It's just, it's just that we . . . It's just that we can't live with ourselves if we don't get somebody's blood on our hands," Lemley said. "Like can you really say that you would just be like, how bad would you feel if you if that just like all that went on, there was . . . a Battle of Richmond and you weren't even fucking there? Wouldn't you feel like a piece of shit? I would definitely be feeling that." ("The Battle of Richmond" was another name for the January 20 gun rally, the "Virginia Plan.")

Mathews: "Sure and to me I don't care if I've shot a bunch of fucking Black kids and something in the back of my fucking head is ringing and it feels bad. I don't fucking care."

Lemley: "I'll do it. I'll do it. I just would be like . . . I'm like aww this sucks. This kid is like whimpering, doesn't understand . . . kid's whimpering, doesn't understand . . . And like it's gonna be really gruesome but fuck it."

As the hours went by, I just kept getting more and more details. The FBI Baltimore team had briefed me before going in about what they needed for the case—certain particular details. But of course, I couldn't just blurt out these questions, so I had to continue playing chess, mentally noting when they would say something that I knew the prosecutors required to piece together the indictment. Everything was playing out perfectly.

When Lemley and Mathews were deep in conversation at one point, I looked directly at one of the cameras hidden in the apartment and winked.

It was the evening of January 11, 2020. The Virginia gun rally was in nine days. The clock was ticking.

I left the apartment and met Rachid and the rest of the Baltimore team at Buffalo Wild Wings, the only place still open. As we sat, about six of us around a table, I handed in my recording gear, and we quickly went through everything that had happened that day.

By the time I got back to my hotel, I only had a couple hours to sleep until my flight the next morning. I needed to get back to Georgia, and fast.

17

FADE TO BLACK

Rome, Georgia
January 12, 2020

I arrived at Lane's farm in the dark, just after 8:30 p.m. I breathed a sigh of relief when I saw Helterbrand's car was still there. After a successful Saturday with Mathews and Lemley, my luck had run out as I tried to get to Georgia the following day.

It started when my flight from Baltimore to Atlanta was hours late. Travel delays are not uncommon and normally are not a big deal, but it felt like every minute mattered as we got closer to the takedown.

The arrests of the first Base members were scheduled for January 15—three days away.

I certainly wasn't the only one working on just a couple of hours of sleep at night for this investigation. In addition to the team tracking the Maryland cell, there was the Atlanta FBI division investigating

Lane, Kaderli, and Helterbrand in Georgia, and there were FBI agents all over the U.S. building cases against Base members in their jurisdictions. Meanwhile, FBI Headquarters was being continually briefed on it all. In these final few days, we needed to make sure none of the Base members acted suddenly, but we also needed to gather what we required for an airtight case. And that meant getting more from Helterbrand, which is why I needed to meet him in Georgia.

After I had convinced Lane to slow down his murder plan so I could gather details about the Antifa couple's home and neighborhood, Helterbrand gave us another delay. He had back surgery on December 27, so he'd asked us to delay the murder a little more so he could recover. I already had Helterbrand on my recordings admitting he had no problem killing "commie kids," but prosecutors would need to show in court that it was more than just talk.

I got out, and as per usual, we left our phones and walked off to talk. Lane had a new idea, that we could make the hit look like someone else killed the couple. He suggested a "MAGA piece of shit." Helterbrand loved this idea.

He had brought to Lanes' farm the four brass catch bags he bought for the killings and the homemade solvent trap suppressor, which would act like a silencer. I was happy to see these items, as they would be important evidence for the prosecutor trying to show Helterbrand had every intention of carrying out the murders.

We went over again everything Lane had told me the last time we discussed the plot, including the fact that it would just be him and Kaderli who would go into the home. But Lane said he had updated the plan, and that we would *all* be going in now. Helterbrand's post would be inside the living room, near a large window to watch outside. Kaderli would be dousing everything with gas, while Lane and I would be clearing the rooms.

Originally, I wasn't supposed to take part in the murders, but Lane believed I had killed before. He said he wanted someone in there with him who had experience. I had never told Lane I had killed, only that I had done and seen a lot of stuff. His mind had done the rest.

Helterbrand wanted to know if fire was needed to cover up any kind of trace we could accidentally leave behind. Lane replied, "Well, that, and also a massive fuck you to them. I mean, it's a pretty big fuck you. Not only are you whacking two people, you're burning their fucking house down." And he started to laugh.

We had not planned on going by the house that night, but Helterbrand asked if we had learned of any alarm systems. I mentioned that, in fact, we had only seen the house in the daytime and maybe it would be good to check it out at night, too? Helterbrand said he was "down," so we loaded up and off we went.

Once again, we talked about how the evening would play out start to finish: Go to the camping location, leave our phones there, go to a dive motel (that hopefully I had paid cash for), clean ourselves, suit up with duct tape securing our clothing, and go kill the couple. We would head back to our camping site after getting rid of our clothing.

Helterbrand's voice came from the back seat. "If at all possible, I would like to pop my cherry."

There was a pause in the conversation. I kept my eyes on the road, then replied, "Which is?"

Lane answered for him. "Well, I think he wants to participate in the fun, too," meaning Helterbrand wanted to put a bullet in the victim's head.

Over this case I had recorded hours and hours of the targets' conversations as we drove or hiked or sat around a campfire or drank under the awning of Lane's family farm. I'll never forget certain phrases. "Pop my cherry" is definitely one of them.

The conversation shifted to the murder weapon we would use. Although a revolver doesn't leave brass, it's rare to find one with a threaded barrel (which we needed to attach a silencer to). Lane and Helterbrand told me that they had decided Lane's .22-caliber semiautomatic pistol would be good for the job.

"Is that enough to get it done?" I asked.

"Yeah. A .22 at that close . . . It'll rattle inside their skull and mix up their brains," Lane said. Then he added, "It'll probably take two or three shots."

I responded, "Then we can all get a shot."

We also talked that night about their plans to murder Mathews and Lemley. They liked the idea of taking their expensive guns and thermal scopes to sell once they were dead. The proceeds would help fund their next murders, and Lane said he had intel coming about possible new targets—"leftist" TV journalists in Tennessee, Georgia, and Alabama.

At one point, Lane recalled a conversation he had had with Mathews. Mathews wanted his advice on what size Crye Precision plate carrier (body armor) he should buy. Lane laughed as he told us he advised Mathews to get a large. He was already thinking about the murder, and so after he was dead, Kaderli could use it. Hey, they joked, maybe we shouldn't kill them yet. Just let them keep stocking up for a few more months. More gear for us!

We all laughed.

I left Lane's farm around 11 p.m.

January 14, 2020

I spent the morning meeting with the SWAT team who would be making Lane's arrest in Georgia. I had to get Lane off his property for the takedown, and we also had to make sure the arrest would take place somewhere remote—to avoid any bystanders being hurt.

The SWAT team predetermined a safe location to do the arrest, not far from Lane's farm. But there was a problem—I had never driven to that area with Lane during the seven-month investigation. There were two ways to turn off the main road as you left Lane's family property. Right, where we always went, which led back to town. And then left, where the SWAT team had decided was the best place for the takedown. I'd have to make sure that wasn't suspicious.

I saw no safety issues as I watched the SWAT team conduct practice runs on a truck similar to mine. But as I listened to members of the SWAT team, I realized the plan included shooting tear gas immediately into my truck through the front windshield—the truck I was going to be stuck driving back to Tennessee; the truck I would be returning to the undercover program after this operation.

As a member of SWAT for many years and a tactical/firearms instructor, I was impressed with their planning, and we ran through a couple of other contingencies. At one point, I pulled the SWAT team leader to the side and said, "I'm not saying I care more about a vehicle than everyone's safety, but . . ."

I confirmed that the main reason for the tear gas or other scenarios was the fact that they wouldn't know if Lane was armed, so I asked, "If I can do my best to guarantee that Lane is unarmed, would that help you?"

He answered, "Yes."

Later that day, I met with Lane to do a face-to-face session with a new Base member that Nazzaro had asked us to vet. This vetting session had already been scheduled and I had to pretend everything was normal. The new recruit was a former U.S. Army medic who was eager to join. The meeting dragged on for hours, until we gave him the green light. "Medic," as he called himself in our chat groups, had no idea what was about to happen to the group he'd just joined (and no idea that he had been hanging out with an FBI agent and someone plotting to murder people).

Driving Lane back to the farm, I started talking about the murders again. I said to him, "Say we got stopped by the cops. Say they found we had guns, even if it was legal. We don't need any attention." I talked about having good OPSEC and suggested it would be a good idea when driving to leave our weapons at home until after the murders.

If Lane was suspicious at all, he didn't show it.

"That's a good idea," he replied.

—

January 15, 2020

I woke up in my Rome, Georgia, hotel room feeling rough. So much was riding on today, but my body was not cooperating. In addition to my back problems, I'd come down with a wicked head cold, which made breathing difficult. Also, due to a food allergy, my stomach was a mess. The night before I had grabbed Applebee's—the only place I could find open near my hotel after I left Lane's farm. They had assured me none of the ingredients that would trigger my allergies were in my meal—they were wrong. I could feel my PTSD kicking in. My breathing was labored and panic was building in my chest.

I called Kara. I just needed to hear her voice. She stayed on the line as I showered and got ready. Just speaking with her made me physically feel better. After I got off the phone, I wiped the condensation from the mirror. All these issues felt like evil attacks from the enemy. I looked at my reflection and said out loud, "Get behind me, Satan! You and all your minions can jump on my back, but I'm crossing the finish line."

I left the hotel room in my white Ford Quad Cab F-150 to pick up Lane for lunch. If all went well, this would be the last time I made the drive to his farm. Even with all my years of experience—undercover work, takedown, car chases—that morning I had butterflies as I drove to pick him up.

Lane got into my truck, and I reminded him of our conversation the night before. "Hey, you're clean, right? You're not carrying?" He assured me he'd left all his weapons at home.

"Cool. Let's go get something to eat."

As I neared the main road, as planned, I turned left. The day before, when we headed out to meet the new prospective member, I had asked Lane where that road led. But Lane didn't have a car and said he didn't know. So now I told him there was a place to eat back that way—I had checked a map—so let's give it a try.

At this point, I was going to fake that something was wrong with my truck, so I had an excuse to pull over. But in a moment of divine intervention, almost on cue, my truck actually made a loud popping sound. "Did you hear that?" I asked him. "I swear, if my brake caliper is frozen again, I'm gonna be pissed!" After driving a bit farther, I said, "I'm going to check it out."

I pulled directly into the spot where the SWAT team wanted me.

I got out, and left Lane in the passenger's seat as I walked around my truck. Seconds later, a Dodge Ram pulled up beside me and a man's voice called out, "Hey, you need some help?"

"Holy shit, dude!" I yelled, walking from my truck. "What the fuck are you doing here? Man, I haven't seen you in forever." Driving the truck was my long-lost "friend," who was really the young FBI case agent from Rome, Georgia (and a former Green Beret), doing his first undercover role. He nailed it!

We now had Lane's full attention, and he turned to look at this stranger.

As Lane stared at us, just over his shoulder I saw the SWAT Bearcat roll over the hill racing toward our truck. A Bearcat is a massive, armored vehicle with a gunner in the turret—something you would picture in Afghanistan or Ukraine, but not in Rome, Georgia. With Lane still watching me and my "friend," I said, "This is a nice truck," and moved toward his Dodge Ram, opening the door.

I saw from my peripheral that the Bearcat was getting close. Boom! I dove into the Dodge Ram, with the agent already behind the wheel, and shouted, "Go! Go! Go!"

We raced away from the scene to the sound of the SWAT team shouting commands.

—

Over the next two days, SWAT teams spread out across Georgia, Delaware, and Wisconsin arresting Base members. Not one shot was fired.

After Lane's arrest, Kaderli was picked up at his home near Atlanta without incident. We had worried that Kaderli's little brother may have been influenced by his big brother. While being questioned with his parents there, he was so nervous he passed out.

At about 5 p.m., Helterbrand was arrested in a parking lot as he left his IT job. Together, all three were charged and held without bail for conspiracy to commit murder, arson, and home invasion (a later charge for animal cruelty would be added for killing the goat). Their phones were confiscated before they could get word out of the takedowns.

As the Georgia crew were arrested, Mathews and Lemley continued to be monitored by the Baltimore FBI team, their every word being recorded. "If I ever get captured, I am going to jail for the rest of my life," Mathews said that day, unaware that the Georgia crew was already in custody. "You realize they're just gonna call us terrorists . . . we're gonna go to jail anyway, might as well go to jail for something good. Might as well do some damage to the system."[1]

Early on January 16, the FBI Baltimore SWAT team descended on Mathews and Lemley's Delaware apartment. Before the agents could get into their apartment, they had both smashed their cellphones and dumped them in the toilet.

Bilbrough was also picked up that day, by the FBI's Washington Field Office's SWAT team, although he would face the least serious offenses of the six.

In Wisconsin, Big Siege, real name Yousef Barasneh, was arrested and charged with vandalism of the synagogue, along with Richard Tobin, a.k.a. Landser, who had called for those assaults on temples and churches.[2] ZoomNat, whose real identity was Duncan Trimmell, and Brandon Ashley, a.k.a. Dema, would also be arrested, months later, for taking part in the Halloween night killing of the goat.

Before his arrest, and writing under the pseudonym of Dema, Ashley wrote a three-thousand-word memoir distancing himself from the group and describing in vivid detail the Halloween killing of "Gar." He released it on the encrypted chat app Telegram, encouraging others not to follow in his footsteps.[3]

He wrote, "I also hold no animosity towards the undercover FBI Agent who infiltrated my cell of the Base. I find it rather courageous he spent his time infiltrating an armed neo-Nazi terrorist cell in the small foothills of the Appalachian mountains in western Georgia."

January 17, 2020

I was back home in Tennessee, but still on the Base Wire chat groups. Nazzaro had deleted Lemley, "Removing @wontgoback temporarily due to an opsec issue." (Lemley had changed his name from "Cantgoback" to "Wontgoback" near the end of the case.) Soon after, someone posted a *Washington Post* story about Lemley's arrest, along with Mathews and Bilbrough.

"If anyone is in contact with Eisen you may want to check up on him," Nazzaro wrote, asking about Bilbrough. News of the Georgia arrests had not yet broken, but those in the chat group—fifty-three members in total—were worried and scrambling for information.

Nazzaro tried to keep them calm. "It means nothing for the rest of us," he wrote. "Don't do anything illegal and you're good to go." He cited passages about perseverance from their book—their bible—*Siege*.

Once more news stories appeared, and court documents became public, the members tried to figure out if there was a snitch or infiltrator. "In reference to paragraph 16 does this mean someone's house was bugged?" wrote one member. "Yes it seems so," Nazzaro replied.

Then he wrote, "Unless someone was wearing a wire of course . . . someone who was there."

They were circling me now, and I remained silent, still reading, still taking frame grabs as evidence.

As Friday went on, the group put more pieces together. News of the Georgia arrests broke. Everyone was trying to figure out who the fed was.

Finally, Nazzaro did.

"He attended every single meetup," he wrote.

"That was probably a red flag in retrospect."

"He put himself out there and went above and beyond."

"There's no way to weed someone like that out easily."

"Actual criminal gangs make people do crimes to prove themselves right? But that option isn't open to us nor should it be," he wrote, knowing he was still being monitored and trying once again to prove The Base was nothing but a survivalist group.

Then I was booted out of the chat group: "Roman has removed you."

I took a screenshot and sent the photo to FBI Headquarters and all the divisions who had worked tirelessly on this case, writing, "And . . . I'm out!"

EPILOGUE

When I retired in June 2021, there was a party for me in my hometown. Friends, family, colleagues, and senior brass from various FBI divisions were all there. It was pretty humbling and emotional seeing so many of the folks who'd made my life what it was over the last thirty years all in the same room.

Having Knox County mayor Glenn Jacobs there was a particular thrill for me. I know him better by his WWE name, "Kane," and for a kid who watched wrestling with his dad ringside every Monday night for six dollars, having Kane in the same room was an incredible retirement gift.

Then Jacobs said, "Come on up. I have a surprise for you."

I responded, "Are you going to choke-slam me through a table?"

"Oh, I don't think you want that," Jacobs said.

But I was actually thinking, *Oh yes, I do! Retiring at fifty and getting choke-slammed through a table by Kane. Check!*

As he read out my bio, I stood beside him, all six-foot-nine and 320 pounds of him. I looked down at the sheet of paper he was holding and skipped ahead to the words that declared June 30 "Scott Payne Day."

I took a deep, slow breath and bit hard on the side of my cheek to try to avoid tearing up on an already emotional day.

As I look back on the sweep of my career, I feel truly blessed by everything that happened, both professionally and personally. I'll never work undercover again, but I'm still working; teaching, speaking, learning, trying to spread knowledge and pay it forward. But not being married to the job also means I have time to fully participate in my real marriage, too.

I wouldn't have been able to do any of this without the support and love of Kara, my girls, and my close-knit Christ-following friends. The stories in this book cover some of the biggest cases I worked on and they're from my perspective. But I didn't work any of these cases alone. None of them would have been possible without an army of talented and hardworking FBI agents, professional staff, and law enforcement partners, who I was proud to work alongside. It wasn't all me. As they say, it takes a village. There are men and women out there who have done way more than I did, and experienced more harrowing encounters than I did, but they aren't getting this attention or credit.

And I know I haven't been easy to work with at times. I'm brash. I rubbed some people the wrong way. Have I been an asshole? Yep. Does my strong personality suck up all the attention and oxygen in a room? Yep. I know I can be a cocky SOB. And I did screw up a lot. But I always believed I was doing the right thing. When I was wrong, I tried to own up to it, and learn from those mistakes.

There's a new, younger generation of agents who have already taken the torch and are running with it. The cream always rises to the top, and I'm thankful for these men and women, because our country still faces so many threats.

In September 2022, I was invited to speak in Pittsburgh at the "Eradicate Hate Global Summit," the second annual anti-hate conference, which began after the 2018 mass shooting at the Tree of Life synagogue in Squirrel Hill, Pittsburgh. Hundreds of participants and speakers came together from all walks of life and political views. There were victims and survivors of hate-fueled crime with devastating stories. There were former white supremacists, jihadis, and other violent extremists who had found their way out, and now work to make sure nobody else follows their path. There were academics and politicians and journalists and lawyers and diplomats. It was my first time presenting in such a public forum since my retirement. I have taught and spoken at some big venues, but they were mainly, if not all, law enforcement. There were a lot of people in that massive conference center in Pittsburgh I never would have encountered in the past. A lot of us were fundamentally different in our politics, upbringing, and outlook on life. But what joined us all was a genuine mission to stop the hate. We talked and, more importantly, we all listened.

It was incredibly motivating.

Then less than a year later, on August 26, 2023, shortly after 1 p.m., a white gunman with a Glock handgun and an AR-15-style rifle with a swastika painted on it walked into a Dollar General store parking lot in Jacksonville, Florida. He unloaded eleven rounds into a car, claiming his first victim. Walking into the store, he shot and killed two more people. All three victims were Black. A white patron in the store was left unharmed. Although he wore a bulletproof vest—seemingly not planning on being killed himself that day—just as officers entered the store they heard a single shot, which they believe was when the gunman killed himself.

The victims were Angela Michelle Carr, who was fifty-two; Anolt Joseph Laguerre Jr., known as A.J., twenty-nine, who worked at the store; and Jerrald De'Shaun Gallion, aged nineteen.[1]

The gunman was twenty-one years old and could have been any of the young men I interacted with while undercover with The Base.

Rinaldo Nazzaro, writing on Telegram as "Roman Wolf," posted after the shooting.

"The problem isn't guns or the internet," he wrote. "The problem is straight White men being deliberately marginalized and alienated in America and falling through the cracks of society as a result. This leads to feelings of anger and hostility which leads to racially motivated lone wolf attacks.[2]

"Therefore, the only solution is establishing an independent sovereign territory for European-Americans where White men will be valued, respected, and honored. Until this happens, the killing will continue."

I don't know how much influence Nazzaro has these days, probably not a lot. But his words are chilling, and there are thousands of white supremacists out there online, posting, reading, and sharing words like that; being radicalized. He's not alone.

I often think of Dr. Martin Luther King's words: "Darkness cannot drive out darkness; only light can do that. Hate cannot drive out hate; only love can do that." I'm not going to wade into the debates about policing except to say I'm saddened by how the badge has been tarnished and how law enforcement is no longer seen as a noble profession by many. But I will say this. There are evil people on this planet who want to do evil things to good people. It's been that way pretty much since the dawn of time. That's where we step in. That's why we're needed. That's why I'm proud of the work I've done, and why I will continue to seek out that light and love.

ACKNOWLEDGMENTS

This acknowledgement section was more difficult than the entire book! It's so hard to narrow down. If I thanked everyone who has helped, backed, and assisted me along the way, it would be its own book.

First and foremost, I must thank the Lord.

For the Eastside High School years, I want to thank Vice Principal Lloyd Walker, Coach Cisson, Coach Simpson, Lamont Smith, and Argentina McGowan. A huge special thanks to the Brew Crüe: Chip Isetts, Ricky Brannen, Don Roddy, Shane Bailey, Tommy Ray (R.I.P.), Shawn Melton, Jody Gentry, and Andrew Culbreath. Our bond is a strong one that has stood the test of time. Love you all!

For the Charleston Southern University years, I want to thank Coach Jacobs, Coach Davis, Coach Dowd, Steve Pilon (a.k.a. Hawk!), and Lee Hargrove (a.k.a. the Boz). A very special thanks to Joe Pharis, who is still my close friend today. We've been through a lot together since 1991.

You have been my barometer and counselor. When I've been weak, you helped me be strong. Love you and the family, brother!

To the bouncing crew, I want to thank Pharis (again), Kevin Felty, and Brian Cox (who introduced me to my wife).

For friendship, guidance, and support at the Greenville County Sheriff's Office, I want to thank John Fouts, Dave Morrow, Gary Ward, Brad Stepp, Rocky Watts, Mike Kellet, Bruce Cannon, and Johnny Mack Brown.

For FBI New York, thanks to Harold Brantley, my 98-17 classmates who accompanied me to New York, Joe Demarest, and the Agents and Task Force Officers of Squad C-23.

For the San Antonio Field Office and McAllen Resident Agency, I want to thank the bosses who supported me and fought for me during the Outlaws case and more. Thank you, U.K. Miller, Aurelio Leal, Steve Ibison, True Brown, and Ralph Diaz. I would also like to thank the agents, Task Force Officers, and analysts who helped me with my cases while I was traveling the country working on many of these undercovers.

For the Knoxville Field Office, thanks to my supporting bosses, John Adams, Mike McLean, Rob Root, Bill Petoskey, Sandra Pollock, Scott Dietsche, Scott Davis, Kieth Paul, Gerry Lyons, Rick Lambert, Ken Moore, Ed Reinhold, and Joe Carrico. For the bosses who I caused extra work for (you know who you are), . . . sorry! For my coworkers on Squads 4 (HIDTA and Safe Streets Task Forces), 9, and 10, thank you. Special thanks to Andy Chapman, Duke Speed, Mike Raliegh, Bryan Martin, Robert Suarez (a.k.a. Bobalu), Sharon Sampson, Tom Joy, and Chad Goins.

To my church family throughout the years, many thanks to Rex Holt, Danny Price, Terry Westerman, Chris Stevens, Michele Stevens, Zac Stephens, Steven DeFur, Mark Beebs, and Brent Ronald. There are way too many worship team/band members to list in this book but know that I love you all! Thanks for the prayers and for keeping me grounded through the good times and bad.

For Operation Roadkill, I must thank the core case team, Thomas Higginbotham, Joe Cummings, Nancy Morelli, Tim Quinn, John Woudenberg, and Peter Levitt. For those of you I met at the award ceremony who were working behind the scenes, I thank you as well. For the cameo crew, I thank Tony, Martin Suarez, Brian Getson, Diego Tobon, Steve Medeiros, and Pete Smith.

For Poetic Justice, I want to thank K.T. Harper, Mark Irwin, Rob Root, Duke Speed, Kelly Kindness, and Steve McFall. On the undercover side, I thank Trucker Paul and Paul B.

For the murder for hires, stolen goods, bombs, and gun cases from Oklahoma to South Carolina, thanks to Craig Overby (98-17!), Grant Lowe, Dave Mackey, Casey Helm, Andy McCabe, and Miles Hutchison.

To the FBI Headquarters Domestic Terrorism and DTOCC crew, I want to thank Cindy Webber, Kate Holden, Khalid Shiraz, Melissa Willig, Tom Nagel, Kari Parker, Matt Hecker, and the numerous DTOS supervisors along the way.

To the multiple teams involved with The Base undercover operation, I thank you all. There are way too many to mention here, but I would like to thank Nathan Plough, Stephanie Shark, Jen Taylor, Scott Penny, Rachid Harrison, Thomas Windom, Sean Burke, Mike Baldino, and Russell Dellinger.

And now to the most diverse motley crew of individuals I have ever been a part of, thank you to the FBI undercover program. I have had so many mentors, peers, and people I've been blessed to mentor, and it's not possible to thank everyone in this section. Thanks to Joe Pistone, Jack Garcia, Steve Salmieri, Lenny Carrol, Bob Bettis, Bob Wittman, Kevin White, Juan Jackson, Mike Chatman, Terry Rankhorn, Mike Henry, DD Dones, Alex Hill, Kenny Ivy, Dave Sebastiani, and Jill Stillman. Thank you to Linda Courtillet for helping me become a better instructor and person. To the Uganda crew, thanks for including me. To the USU crew, I want to thank Meredith Krause, Nicole Cruz, Ric Seabrooks (Elvis wouldn't be

Elvis!), John Kohler, Oscar Jiminez, Glenda Smith, Chris Ferrer, and Jean Fanelli. Thanks to my brothers, J. Cooper, Trucker Paul, Shaun McAlpin, and Brian Getson. For all their support and guidance, a special thanks to Mark Horton, Barry "Bo" Loggins, and Don Yarbrough (a.k.a. Bandit).

For the individuals who helped me get to this point post FBI, I would like to thank John Black, Richie Walls, Brian Conley, Craig Gore, Phil Donlon, Matt Ochacher, and the illustrious Paul Solotaroff, who did such an amazing job with my *Rolling Stones* magazine article (and hounded the *you know what* out of me to meet my literary agents for this book). To think this all started because of my connection to professional wrestling. Thanks, Mayor Kane (a.k.a. Glenn Jacobs)!

And, furthermore, I would like to give thanks to all the First Responders. Thank you for being on the wall.

To the book team, a huge thank you to literary agents Larry Weissman and Sascha Alper for taking a chance on me and believing in this project. To my co-writer Michelle Shephard, thanks for putting up with me during this entire process. To editor Amar Deol, I remember pitching several editors. You were the only one that picked up on my faith (as a Christ follower) and asked me about it. Then you said you would love to see that throughout the book. When I closed my laptop from that Zoom call, I knew you were the one! To editor Yaniv Soha, thanks for getting this baby across the finish line. And to Hannah Frankel and anyone else I failed to mention at Atria or Simon and Schuster, please know that you are greatly appreciated.

As I said in the epilogue, I also want to thank my wife and my daughters. I lost a lot of time with them as I poured my heart and soul into my job, and I'm happy to be there for them fully now. Thanks to my mom and dad for instilling the values, work ethic, and morals I still have today.

ABOUT THE AUTHORS

Scott Payne is a retired FBI Special Agent who spent twenty-eight years in law enforcement investigating cases against drug- and human-trafficking organizations, human traffickers, outlaw motorcycle clubs, gangs, public corruption, and domestic terrorism. He was also a SWAT team operator and instructor for firearms, tactics, and undercover operations. He lives in the Southeast with his wife, two daughters, and dogs.

Michelle Shephard is an award-winning journalist, author, and filmmaker who covered terrorism, national security, and civil rights for two decades as a correspondent with *The Toronto Star*. Her career has taken her around the world, including multiple reporting trips to Somalia, Yemen, Pakistan, and Guantanamo Bay. She is based in Toronto with her photojournalist husband and her dog, Parker.

A NOTE ON SOURCES

The anecdotes and stories contained in this book are based on personal recollections, contemporaneous notes, emails and text messages, public records, and other sources. Where notes or records did not exist for a particular conversation, we have reconstructed the exchange to the very best of our recollections. Where portions of books or articles are quoted, we have so acknowledged. The names of some people portrayed in the book have been changed.

NOTES

PROLOGUE

1. Pseudonym

CHAPTER FOUR: RUNNING ON EMPTY

1. "FBI—Houston Division press release," FBI, October 23, 2009. https://archives.fbi.gov/archives/houston/press-releases/2009/ho102309.htm.
2. Robert D. McFadden, "Motorcyclist Is Fatally Shot on Interstate in Connecticut," *New York Times,* April 3, 2006. https://www.nytimes.com/2006/04/03/nyregion/motorcyclist-is-fatally-shot-on-interstate-in-connecticut.html.
3. Carson Walker, "Hells Angels Bikers to Admit South Dakota Charges," Associated Press, February 3, 2009. https://www.sandiegouniontribune.com/sdut-sd-biker-shooting-020309-2009feb03-story.html.

CHAPTER FIVE: THE BASEMENT

1. *USA. v. Noe et al.*, United States District Court, Massachusetts (2007), Exhibit "302," report by FBI Special Agent Scott Payne, regarding September 8, 2006 incident (transcribed September 9, 2015).

CHAPTER SIX: THE CRASH

1. *USA. v. Noe et al.*, United States District Court, Massachusetts (2007), Exhibit

"302," report by FBI Special Agent Scott Payne, regarding a November 30, 2006, incident (transcribed December 4, 2006).

2. "Audit of the Federal Bureau of Investigation's National Security Undercover Operations," FBI, December 2022. https://oig.justice.gov/sites/default/files/reports/23-012.pdf ; Joe Davidson, "Safety Training Lapses Endanger FBI Undercover Agents, Watchdog Says," *Washington Post*, January 13, 2023, https://www.washingtonpost.com/politics/2023/01/13/fbi-undercover-operatives-training-safety-watchdog/.
3. *USA v. Timothy J. Silvia*, United States District Court, Massachusetts (2007), Exhibit in Support of Defendant's Sentencing Memorandum and Motion for Departure Pursuant to USSG § 4A1.3 (B) (1); *USA v. Timothy J. Silvia*, United States District Court, Massachusetts (2007), Docket 130-1-Redacted Transcript (October 21, 2008).

CHAPTER SEVEN: MARLBORO MAN

1. Jo C. Goode, "Outlaws Member Found Not Guilty in 2019 Fall River Biker Brawl Murder," *Herald News*, September 2, 2022. https://www.heraldnews.com/story/news/courts/2022/09/02/outlaws-biker-club-member-found-not-guilty-biker-brawl-shooting/7964197001/.
2. United States Census Bureau. https://www.census.gov/quickfacts/unioncountytennessee.
3. Thomas Francis, "How Florida Brothers' 'Pill Mill' Operation Fueled Painkiller Abuse Epidemic," NBC News. https://www.nbcnews.com/news/world/how-florida-brothers-pill-mill-operation-fueled-painkiller-abuse-epidemic-flna757480.
4. Centers for Disease Control and Prevention, National Center for Health Statistics, Press Release, May 11, 2022. https://www.cdc.gov/nchs/pressroom/nchs_press_releases/2022/202205.htm.

CHAPTER EIGHT: PILL SICK

1. Faith Karimi, "These Florida brothers ran one of the largest opioid 'pill mills' in U.S. history. The FBI says it was linked to thousands of deaths," CNN, February 3, 2003. https://www.cnn.com/2023/02/03/us/american-pain-pill-mill-documentary-cec/index.html.
2. HHS Office of Inspector General, "Opioid Use in Medicare Part D in States in the Appalachian Region." https://oig.hhs.gov/reports-and-publications/workplan/summary/wp-summary-0000354.asp (retrieved November 1, 2023).
3. Kentucky Injury Prevention and Research Center, "Drug Overdose Deaths in Kentucky, 2000–2015," July 2016. https://kiprc.uky.edu/sites/default/files/2020-12/OD-deaths-ky-residents-2000-2015.pdf.
4. *USA v. Devault*, Eastern District of Tennessee, Knoxville (2008), Plea Agreement.
5. Cooke-Campbell-Mortuary, Inc., Obituary Jay Michael "Mike" Collins. https://www.cooke-campbellmortuary.com/memorials/Collins-Jay-Michael/4204193/.

CHAPTER NINE: I RECKON I GOT A LITTLE BIT OF HATRED

1. *USA v. Benjamin McDowell*, U.S. District Court, South Carolina (2017-02-16), Criminal Complaint.
2. Michael S. Schmidt, "Background Check Flaw Let Dylann Roof Buy Gun, FBI Says," *New York Times*, July 10, 2015. https://www.nytimes.com/2015/07/11/us/background-check-flaw-let-dylann-roof-buy-gun-fbi-says.html.
3. "Statement by FBI Director James Comey Regarding Dylann Roof Gun Purchase," FBI, July 10, 2015. https://www.fbi.gov/news/press-releases/statement-by-fbi-director-james-comey-regarding-dylann-roof-gun-purchase.
4. Rachel Kaadzi Ghansah, "A Most American Terrorist: The Making of Dylann Roof," *GQ*, August 21, 2017. https://www.gq.com/story/dylann-roof-making-of-an-american-terrorist; "Hate Symbol: Bowlcut/Dylann Roof," Anti-Defamation League, https://www.adl.org/resources/hate-symbol/bowlcutdylann-roof.
5. "Aryan Nations," Southern Poverty Law Center. https://www.splcenter.org/fighting-hate/extremist-files/group/aryan-nations.
6. Aaron Ladd and Audrey Biesk, "Family says man sentenced to prison for planning 'Dylann Roof-style' attack is not prejudiced," WMBF News, July 11, 2018. https://www.wmbfnews.com/story/38621371/family-says-man-sentenced-to-prison-for-planning-dylann-roof-style-attack-is-not-prejudiced/.

CHAPTER TEN: THE KLAN BAND

1. "Ku Klux Klan," Southern Poverty Law Center. https://www.splcenter.org/fighting-hate/extremist-files/ideology/ku-klux-klan.
2. "Federal Grand Jury Indicts 44 Individuals in Methamphetamine Distribution Conspiracy," United States Attorney's Office, Eastern District of Tennessee Press Release, March 26, 2018. https://www.justice.gov/usao-edtn/pr/federal-grand-jury-indicts-44-individuals-methamphetamine-distribution-conspiracy.
3. Saphora Smith, "Aryan Nations gang member shot Tennessee Officer captured, police say," *NBC News and Associated Press*, January 12, 2018. https://www.nbcnews.com/news/us-news/aryan-nations-gang-member-shot-tennessee-officer-loose-police-say-n837216.

CHAPTER ELEVEN: I KNOW A GUY

1. *USA v. Aleshia Hope Stuart*, United State District Court Eastern District of Tennessee Greeneville Division, July 30, 2015, Criminal Complaint.
2. Nelson Morais, "Murder-for-Hire Suspect Signs Plea Agreement for Eight-Year Sentence," *Newport Plain Talk*, June 16, 2015. https://www.newportplaintalk.com/news/article_caf46e30-141f-11e5-a0ab-e7aaeca136d1.html.
3. Christine Holmes, "Somerset Couple Sentenced in Murder Conspiracy," *Zanesville Times Recorder*, December 16, 2020. https://www.zanesvilletimesrecorder.com/story/news/2020/12/16/somerset-couple-sentenced-murder-conspiracy/3920389001/.

CHAPTER TWELVE: SAVE YOUR RACE, JOIN THE BASE

1. "Atomwaffen Division," Southern Poverty Law Center. https://www.splcenter.org/fighting-hate/extremist-files/group/atomwaffen-division.
2. Ben Makuch and Mack Lamoureaux, "Neo-Nazis Are Organizing Secretive Paramilitary Training Across America," *Vice,* November 20, 2018. https://www.vice.com/en/article/a3mexp/neo-nazis-are-organizing-secretive-paramilitary-training-across-america.
3. Jason Wilson, "Revealed: The True Identity of the Leader of an American Neo-Nazi Terror Group," *Guardian,* January 24, 2020. https://www.theguardian.com/world/2020/jan/23/revealed-the-true-identity-of-the-leader-of-americas-neo-nazi-terror-group?CMP=Share_iOSApp_Other&__twitter_impression=true; Wilson, "Revealed." Ibid.
4. Daniel De Simone, Andrei Soshnikov and Ali Winston, "Neo-Nazi Rinaldo Nazzaro running US militant group The Base from Russia," *BBC,* January 24, 2020, https://www.bbc.com/news/world-51236915.
5. Ryan Thorpe, "Homegrown Hate," *Winnipeg Free Press,* June 12, 2019 (modified October 15, 2021). https://www.winnipegfreepress.com/featured/2019/06/12/homegrown-hate-2.
6. Sara J. Bloomfield, "White Supremacists Are Openly Using Nazi Symbols," *Washington Post,* August 22, 2017. https://www.washingtonpost.com/news/posteverything/wp/2017/08/22/white-supremacists-are-openly-using-nazi-symbols-thats-a-warning-to-all-of-us/; Joe Heim, "This White Nationalist Who Shoved a Trump Protestor May Be the Next David Duke," *Washington Post,* April 12, 2016. https://www.washingtonpost.com/local/this-white-nationalist-who-shoved-a-trump-protester-may-be-the-next-david-duke/2016/04/12/7e71f750-f2cf-11e5-89c3-a647fcce95e0_story.html.
7. "Truck of former reservist with alleged neo-Nazi ties found near U.S.-Canada border," CBC News, September 3, 2019. https://www.cbc.ca/news/canada/manitoba/patrik-mathews-truck-base-1.5268780.

CHAPTER THIRTEEN: HATE CAMPS

1. Author interview, Michelle Shephard and Terry Rankhorn.
2. Benjamin Wallace, "The Prep-School Nazi," *New York,* March 30, 2020. https://nymag.com/intelligencer/2020/03/rinaldo-nazzaro-the-base-norman-spear.html.
3. Committee on Homeland Security, House of Representative Hearing, September 10, 2019. https://www.govinfo.gov/content/pkg/CHRG-116hhrg39837/pdf/CHRG-116hhrg39837.pdf.
4. "Kristallnacht," Holocaust Encyclopedia. https://encyclopedia.ushmm.org/content/en/article/kristallnacht.
5. *USA v. Richard Tobin,* United States District Court, New Jersey, November 12, 2019, Criminal Complaint. https://www.documentcloud.org

/documents/6550995-Richard-Tobin-Criminal-Complaint (retrieved November 2, 2023).

6. Ibid.

CHAPTER FOURTEEN: THE WILD HUNT

1. "The Wild Hunt," Norse Mythology. https://norse-mythology.org/the-wild-hunt/ (retrieved November 2, 2023).
2. *USA v. Brian Lemley Jr. and Patrik Jordan Mathews*, United States District Court, Maryland, 2020, Government's Memorandum in Aid of Sentencing.

CHAPTER FIFTEEN: THE CAMPING TRIP

1. *The State v. Michael John Helterbrand, Jacob Oliver Kaderli, Luke Austin Lane*, Superior Court of Said County, Floyd County, Georgia, 2021, Affidavit of Sergeant Matt Meyers, Floyd County PD.
2. Kara Berg, "White Supremacist Group Leader Sentenced for Terrorizing Dexter Family, AG's Office Says," *Detroit News*, August 18, 2022. https://www.detroitnews.com/story/news/local/wayne-county/2022/08/18/white-supremacist-group-leader-sentenced-terrorizing-dexter-family/10357241002/.
3. *The State v. Michael John Helterbrand, Jacob Oliver Kaderli, Luke Austin Lane*, "Affidavit."

CHAPTER SIXTEEN: THE BOOGALOO

1. *USA v. Brian Lemley Jr. and Patrik Jordan Mathews*, United States District Court, Maryland, 2020, Government's Memorandum in Aid of Sentencing.
2. *USA v. Brian Lemley Jr. and Patrik Jordan Mathews*, United States District Court, Maryland, 2020, Government's Response to Defense Sentencing Memorandum.
3. Casey Michel, "Want to Meet America's Worst Racists? Come to the Northwest," *Politico*, July 7, 2015. https://www.politico.com/magazine/story/2015/07/northwest-front-americas-worst-racists-119803/.
4. *USA v. Brian Lemley Jr. and Patrik Jordan Mathews*, "Government's Memorandum in Aid of Sentencing."
5. "The Extremist Medicine Cabinet: A Guide to Online 'Pills,'" Anti-Defamation League. https://www.adl.org/resources/blog/extremist-medicine-cabinet-guide-online-pills.
6. *USA v. Brian Lemley Jr. and Patrik Jordan Mathews*, Government's Memorandum in Aid of Sentencing.
7. Graham Moomaw, "'Madam Speaker': After 400 years, Filler-Corn Becomes First Woman to Lead Virginia House," *Virginia Mercury*, January 8, 2020. https://www.virginiamercury.com/2020/01/08/madame-speaker-after-400-years-filler-corn-becomes-first-woman-to-lead-virginia-house/.
8. Alexandra Alter, "How 'The Turner Diaries' Incites White Supremacists," *New*

York Times, January 12, 2021. https://www.nytimes.com/2021/01/12/books/turner-diaries-white-supremacists.html.

CHAPTER SEVENTEEN: FADE TO BLACK

1. *USA v. Brian Lemley Jr. and Patrik Jordan Mathews*, United States District Court, Maryland, 2020, Government's Memorandum in Aid of Sentencing.
2. "Oak Creek Man Who Vandalized Racine Synagogue Pleads Guilty," United States Attorney's Office, Eastern District of Wisconsin, Press Release, August 13, 2020. https://www.justice.gov/usao-edwi/pr/oak-creek-man-who-vandalized-racine-synagogue-pleads-guilty; Paul Solotaroff, "He Spent 25 Years Infiltrating Nazis, the Klan and Biker Gangs," *Rolling Stone*, January 30, 2022. https://www.rollingstone.com/culture/culture-features/fbi-infiltrator-nazis-kkk-biker-gangs-1280830/.
3. Ben Makuch and Mack Lamoureux, "Members of Neo-Nazi Org The Base Indicted for Sacrificing Ram While on Acid," *Vice*, April 16, 2021. https://www.vice.com/en/article/akgzda/members-of-neo-nazi-org-the-base-indicted-for-sacrificing-ram-while-on-acid.

EPILOGUE

1. Livia Albeck-Ripka, Anna Betts, Orlando Mayorquin, Nichole Manna, and Patricia Mazzei, "What to Know About the Jacksonville Shooting," *New York Times*, August 27, 2023. https://www.nytimes.com/2023/08/27/us/jacksonville-shooting-dollar-general.html.
2. Rinaldo Nazzaro posting as @RomanWolf on Telegram, August 26, 2023.

INDEX